WITH
every thing in four pictures

by Andrea Edin

With

Cover Design and artwork by Andrea Edin

Published by Radiant Publishing
Paperback ISBN: 979-8-9865413-1-0
eISBN: 979-8-9865413-2-7

First Edition

Printed in the United States

"Then Jesus took them through the writings
of Moses and all the prophets,
explaining from all the Scriptures
the things concerning himself."

Luke 24:27 NLT

Table of Contents

INTRODUCTION

Searching High and Low

At the close of his storied life, Moses climbed the slopes of Mount Pisgah. From that summit, God showed him the lay of the Promised Land. Horizon to horizon, it stretched beneath and beyond him, blessed in every direction. For forty years, he had wandered through the baking wilderness dreaming of this moment. At last, he could see the carved ridges and fertile plains, the cool rivers and glistening seas that made up Israel's God-given homeland. In one glorious, wide-sweeping vista, he drank it all in.

Paul had a similar moment when he picked up his pen to write to the church in Ephesus. What began quietly turned into a cataract of sheer wonder. The first chapter of Ephesians builds into a soaring chorus. You can hear the sound of Paul's eyes widening before the greatness of God's mad plan. It is the song of his overjoyed heart searching for the bottom as he was inundated with grace, his spirit trying to catch its breath as he laid out all he had witnessed. His pen was scratching furiously, just trying to keep up. By the time he got ahold of himself, he was already in chapter four.

Perhaps you have been on such a hike. The slog of climbing through the tree cover and brush shields you from the view, and the change in elevation is so gradual you do not even sense it. But then chance comes when the trees thin and the clouds lift, and you turn around. There is nothing but open heaven and vast earth before you, and a panorama to leave you speechless. What just a moment before was familiar and small is now enormous, limitless, and shimmeringly beautiful. That is what happened to Peter, John, and James at the Transfiguration.

But Moses assures us a view like this is not limited to spiritual mountaintops or giants in the faith. It is closer to us than we can imagine. As he put it:

> *"It is not beyond your reach. It is not kept in heaven, so distant that you must ask, 'Who will go up to heaven and bring it down so we can hear it and obey?' It is not kept beyond the sea, so far away that you must ask, 'Who will cross the sea to bring it to us so we can hear it and obey?' No, the message is very close at hand; it is on your lips and in your heart so that you can obey it."*[1]

This panorama is woven into the Scriptures, where every page and every word are brimming with grace and glory. Only look, leaning on the Holy Spirit to guide you as a Sherpa, and you will see it. He promises those who search will not walk away disappointed. Everyone who seeks finds.

What you will see is Jesus. You will begin to see the outline of His face and His hands, His eyes and His hair, His frame and His feet. You will see His picture again and again across the Bible's many books and stories, and it will dawn on you that He is the only character God has written about. You will understand what is meant by, "Your word is a lamp for my feet, a light on my path,"[2] for you know Who the way we travel is. The lamplight floods Him. You will grasp then that Jesus is Christ crucified. That is the only message the Word declares. You will see Him exactly as He is because God so desires it for you. The Holy Spirit will help you. He will sit with you as you turn the pages of the photo album, pointing Jesus out in all His beauty.

The disciples once asked Jesus, "Rabbi, where are You staying?"[3] The answer is that you will find Him in the most surprising places. He is in the Prophets and the Psalms. He is in the Law. You will find Him with the infant church, in Rome's harsh dungeons, and all throughout Paul's letters, and you will find Him as He walks the humble streets of Galilee and Jerusalem. He is in Egypt and Babylon, the heights of heaven, the desert, and the depths of the sea.

You will find Him in the past. You will find Jesus at the foundation of the universe, there before all other things. He is the One who was, for He became a man and died. He was. You will also find Him farther ahead, for He is the One who will be. He is there already at the end. He, the Living God, once lay in a tomb, waiting for life to begin again. And now He is! Life came roaring back into His bones so that death could no longer have any power over us.

You will find Him with the sick, bedridden, and with widows and fishermen. You will find Him with lepers and shepherds and little children. You will find Him in floods and famines, in the times of war and wandering. He is there in the royal courts and under the cover of the Holy of Holies. The train of His robe fills the temple, and He knows each star by name.

"Where are You staying, Rabbi?" the disciples asked.

He is with us. Yes, open your eyes and take in the full view. In Jesus's own words, dear child: "Come and you will see."[4] It is His invitation to start the search.

Don't miss this first command Jesus gave. Before He invited His disciples to follow, before He sent them to preach or to heal or to baptize or to love, Jesus required them to look so that they might learn to see—to see Him. Let us do the same. Linger until He comes into view and your heart catches fire.

Mary, mother to Jesus, was present when a knock shook the front door of her home one day. She opened it to find a group of strangers waiting on the step. They had traveled for hundreds of miles from some foreign country in the hopes of an audience with her child.

She courteously let them inside. Her baby was just learning to walk, a little toddler babbling happily and drooling when He smiled. She watched them drop to their knees in reverence at the sight of Him.

They opened up packs strapped to the animals they'd ridden across the continent and laid out riches that must have made her catch her breath. Gold coins, expensive myrrh resin, and fragrant, finely ground incense were set before Jesus in worship. Mary had no idea who these men were or why they were here to visit. She had no idea how they had even found her young family, as she and Joseph were just in Bethlehem for a temporary stay.

Most likely, the men did not know fully either. They were astrologers by trade and belonged to some other ancient faith, neither Jews by creed nor by ethnicity. They had no known connection to the land of Israel or its history. They were scholars and made it their business to search the stars' trails and planetary orbits for insight.

We are so familiar with seeing the Wise Men in our nativity sets that we forget they had no reason whatsoever to seek Jesus out. Why should they care that Israel had an heir to the throne? Why should they visit and exalt

Him with gifts? What was Israel to them, or Israel's God for that matter? Imagine Mary's curiosity when she saw them at the door.

But God knew. Their timely arrival was His doing. He had secretly but deliberately invaded their sphere. One night, He hung a special star in the heavens, speaking their academic dialect to grab their attention. He knew they would be looking, and the effect was like Copernicus reorienting the planets around the sun. Suddenly, everything in the skies had a new slant and a new interpretation. They saw it rising in the east, this burning star that gave meaning to every other constellation they thought they understood. It was a sign only astrologers could take note of, and it dramatically diverted their course. Right away, they set out for Jerusalem to find the one this star spoke of. They knew it was a birth announcement of huge significance, of a great king who deserved their worship.

God had arranged for this moment billions of years before when He set the galaxies in their place and gave the stars the word to blaze their light. And at just the right moment, His Christ finally came. The heavens were in perfect position to announce Him. "Come and see!" they beckoned.

God had told Isaiah to watch for it:

> *"Arise, Jerusalem! Let your light shine for all to see. For the glory of the Lord rises to shine on you. Darkness as black as night covers all the nations of the earth, but the glory of the Lord rises and appears over you. All nations will come to your light; mighty kings will come to see your radiance. Look and see, for everyone is coming home! Your sons are coming from distant lands; your little daughters will be carried home. Your eyes will shine, and your heart will thrill with joy, for merchants from around the world will come to you. They will bring you the wealth of many lands. Vast caravans of camels will converge on you, the camels of Midian and Ephah. The people of Sheba will bring gold and frankincense and will come worshipping the Lord. The flocks of Kedar will be given to you, and the rams of Nebaioth will be brought for my altars. I will accept their offerings, and I will make my Temple glorious."*[5]

The Wise Men had traveled first to Jerusalem, naturally expecting a prince would be born in the royal palace. But when they spoke with King Herod, he was deeply alarmed. Jesus was obviously not his son and not his heir. Afraid a rebellion was brewing against his dynasty, Herod worked quickly. He pretended to be devout and gathered as much information as he could from the foreigners regarding Jesus's exact whereabouts. In reality, he was planning to kill this baby.

The king instructed the astrologers to continue on to Bethlehem where the ancient prophets had promised the Messiah would be. He pointed them to Scripture and unwittingly gave them advice that we who love Him should also wholeheartedly follow: "Go and search carefully for the child. As soon as you find him, report to me, so that I too may go and worship him."[6]

This is what all Bible study, all spiritual discipline, all prayer, fasting, and wisdom, all waiting for God to speak and to move boil down to. Search for the Child. Search carefully for Him. Search for Him in the rustling pages of Scripture, and in quiet moments alone in God's presence, and in the louder ones gathered together with His people. Always be searching. Do not stop until you have found Him, no matter what page you are on or what spiritual atmosphere surrounds you. He is there, but He must be sought, and you must not let up until you have Him in sight. Don't stop short. And once you find Him, worship Him! Lift that missing Lamb up around your shoulders, call your friends together, and break open the best wine in the house.

The Wise Men were well rewarded for their efforts. They bowed down and offered their peculiar baby gifts, which by God's prescient brilliance shed light on who this wondrous little Child truly was: incense to mark His priestly intercession on the cross, myrrh to embalm His body for burial, and gold to form the luminous crown He would receive at resurrection.

Seek the Christ—patiently, intentionally, lovingly—and you will see Him too.

The pages that follow lay out many stories from Scripture, some very well-known and beloved, others less familiar, but they are by no means exhaustive. There are a thousand more the Spirit would love to open up! The ones contained here are arranged under four major metaphors that run through the Testaments like silver veins in the hillsides. The Holy Spirit is an excellent teacher, and He knows that if we are to understand the words of the Bible, we need to look at the pictures. These metaphors are His illustrations so we can grasp all the Father revealed through His Christ, the wonderful, mysterious things no eye could see and no mind could conceive of before that first Easter. He has so much He wants to tell us. He is on a God-given mission, remember. He was sent to glorify Jesus and lead us into all truth.

The four metaphors are sea, ground, robe and child. They are common enough for us to know by touch, sight and smell, and they are His tools to exalt Jesus. May Christ become so brilliant in our eyes, yours and mine, that we see no one and nothing else. The Holy Spirit assures us He is up to the task.

---

1 Deuteronomy 30:11–14 NLT
2 Psalms 119:105 NIV
3 John 1:38 NLT
4 John 1:39 NIV
5 Isaiah 60:1–7
6 Matthew 2:8

Picture One: *Sea*

CHAPTER ONE

Wind and Waves

"When you go through deep waters,
I will be with you.
When you go through rivers of difficulty,
you will not drown."

– Isaiah 43:2 NLT

Our story begins at the waterline, right where the lake quietly ripples up to the shore. Luke tells us it was a fine morning. The sun was just rising over the Sea of Galilee, and a hunched-over Peter was silhouetted against it in the shallows.[1]

He was a fisherman. He and his partners were scrubbing out nets and packing up. Their boats bobbed gently on the lake, and cheerful birdsong filled the air. But Peter's mood was far from idyllic. He grabbed the gear and pitched it hard onto the sand. It fell with a dull thud, echoing the frustrated dullness they all felt to see the sun coming up. No one had caught a thing after a full night out on the water. Tired, hungry, and empty-handed, they decided to call it quits and return home.

A few steps down the beach, they overheard a commotion. Peter looked up as he tied off the boat and gathered the last of his things. People suddenly began to descend on the lake in droves, trailing behind a single figure. That man, Peter recognized, was the famous Rabbi Jesus. Jesus was speaking to the crowd as they pressed in close.

But to his surprise, Jesus paused and waded over in Peter's direction. He went straight out to one of their fishing boats and asked Peter if He could borrow it. He wanted to teach from it. The crowd had pushed in so tightly they left Him no room to stand on the beach. He also asked if Peter wouldn't mind rowing Him out a few yards.

Peter was worn out, but he was a kind and good-natured man. He agreed. He set the nets down, picked up an oar, and got back into the water.

He climbed into the boat where Jesus was already waiting for Him. They pushed out a bit from shore, and the size of the vast crowd hit him. Peter silently studied their faces. They were spellbound as they listened to their Teacher. He looked at Jesus while He talked on and on and then over at his partners, still patiently waiting for the chance to go home. Idly, he watched the sun climb higher and burn warmer in the sky.

At last, Jesus finished and sent the people away. Peter started rowing back to the beach, but Jesus stopped him. "Now let's go out where the water is deeper," He said. "Fish out there."

With that, the last ounce of politeness drained from Peter. His cheeks grew hot and his pulse rose. Fishing was his job, and the Sea of Galilee might as well have been his backyard. No one knew this lake like he did or how better to profit from it. He hadn't slept, hadn't eaten, and had certainly been more than courteous toward Jesus's demands on his time.

"Master," he said in exasperation, "we've worked hard all night and caught nothing." He motioned toward James and John and the others. If there were fish to catch, they of all people would have hauled them in by now.

But as he spoke, something flickered through him and told him to trust Jesus on this. He shook his head wearily, half believing what he was about to do next.

"All right." He sighed. "Because You say so, I'll do it. Let's fish."

He turned around and headed out to a deep section of the lake. No sooner had he thrown the net overboard than the water began to thrash and boil foamy white. Hundreds of fish darted toward the net, and soon there were so many he couldn't lift it out. It began to rip under the immense weight. He shouted back to shore for James and John to come help. Adrenaline replaced fatigue, followed by panic. The boat was on the verge of capsizing.

The others came, and soon both boats were filled to the brim. Peter looked over at Jesus in a mix of awe and terror. He fell to his knees. Waters that were dead just moments ago were now teeming with life.

Sprawled on the deck, surrounded by the staccato of flopping fish, he begged Jesus to leave and let him be. Holiness like this had no business in Peter's little life.

Nothing could have been further from Jesus's mind.

Our story begins at the water because that is where God always begins. Genesis paints the same imagery for us as Luke. There was chaos and emptiness at the very beginning in the form of a black sea. Deep darkness shrouded those even deeper waters. There was no life in them, no light or purpose, and Scripture makes no mention of how they got there.[2]

What it does tell us is that the beginning came when God rebuked those waters and commanded everything to change. He spoke, a cowboy bridling a mustang, and they instantly submitted. At His word, light appeared, and life circulated through the waters like sunbeams streaking through the surface, for life is the will of God. Life filled the waters. Life exploded out of the waters and covered the horizons. Life surged into the sea and the skies like an electric current, and the waters began to burst with vivid, vibrant color.

"Swarm, Ocean, with fish and all sea life!"[3] God sang happily. "Men and women, my most Beloved, you are going to rule here!" Fish flooded into the sea and birds soared into the waters above. That dark, dead chaos was unrecognizably transformed. He had overthrown death, and the story could start.

How had it happened? By His word and through His presence. The Father was there at the beginning, His Spirit hovering over the surface of the water, and His Son with us as the Word. And when God is with us, like a chemical reaction, the effect is always life.

Luke leaves little doubt for us who this Speaker at the lake had to be or what He had authority to do. Peter saw it too, and it frightened him nearly out of his skin. The Creator was there doing what He had done all along: reigning over the sea. He was putting life into dead things on a colossal level.

Yet the Holy Spirit prompted Luke to pay attention to Peter too, for this is humanity's history as much as it is God's. Peter's discouragement from the night of bad fishing and terror of an unveiled Jesus marks the gulf between God and our tiny, fragile lives, for we have a very different relationship with death. Death is a brutal tyrant lording its will over humanity. It crushes us and takes what is most dear. We all know it will come for each of us, someday, though we do our best to resist. All Peter could do was bow in the face of defeat.

The struggle with the sea we call death is not unique to down-on-their-luck fishermen. The metaphor runs all through Scripture because it is the singular human condition. These dark and unruly waters are calamity, despair, overwhelming trouble, and the grave. The Psalms lament over fearsome currents that rise and knock our feet out from under us. We all fight to keep our head above the waves, treading furiously, hope against hope, crying out for rescue. Far too well-acquainted with them, David once wept on the run from his enemies, saying:

> *"Save me, O God, for the floodwaters are up to my neck. Deeper and deeper I sink into the mire; I can't find a foothold. I am in deep water, and the floods overwhelm me. Pull me from these deep waters. Don't let the floods overwhelm me, or the deep waters swallow me, or the pit of death devour me."*[4]

Paul also had plenty of reason to fear a high tide. He had been starved, robbed and rejected throughout his missionary work. More than once, he was shipwrecked in his travels. Fierce storms sank vessels out from beneath him, leaving him adrift in the open ocean and stranded on strange coasts. He faced death daily as he pressed on, some days valiantly and some not sure he would live to see another.

King Jehoshaphat could only watch as his entire fleet of trading ships broke up at sea, taking the crew and all his wealth down to the bottom. Job learned that Leviathan lurked just past the shoals and could snatch up everything precious in a moment. Moses, whose name literally means "Lifted from the waters," trusted his tiny frame to a basket on the crocodile-infested Nile. And I think we can certainly forgive Noah and Jonah if neither wanted to see another boat again in their lives.

As the sun rose over the Sea of Galilee, Peter was doing his darndest to get away from the water. His struggle had lasted all through the night against it, but he had lost, and all that he could do now was accept it. That is ultimately all any of us can do when it comes to death. But the Jesus he encountered seemed to be on an entirely different plane. He had no fear of the sea. He wanted in. He waded out willingly and even beckoned Peter to join Him, and then proceeded to wring every last drop of hidden treasure from those awful waters.

Peter collapsed before Jesus, scared to death of Him as much as death itself. Who has power like this? He knew it was God at work. What he did not yet know was there was absolutely no reason to be afraid. Jesus had just revealed what He planned to do to death, down to the most minute detail. He would throttle it, plunder it, and destroy it for good. It would all come about by Him stepping first into the waters. By the time Peter and the rest of us heard His call to follow suit, the sea would be tame under His hand.

The grandness of the scope and scale of Jesus's saving work was far beyond what Peter could grasp at the moment. He saw God in Jesus's super abilities, but they only made Him seem more alien and distant. Jesus had triumphed easily where Peter stumbled. There was no overlap Peter could find between this holy miracle man and himself.

It meant that Jesus would have to try again to win over his trust, a dare Jesus was very glad to take him up on. At His request, Peter left his boat that day, curious enough to follow Jesus on land and into ministry. He dropped his nets on the beach and walked away from his family business. Maybe he was even a little glad to be rid of it. Soon enough, though, Jesus would have him back out on the water.

Some months afterward, Jesus ordered His disciples to sail across the Sea of Galilee. The day had been a flurry of teaching, crowd wrangling, and feasting. But night was falling and Jesus told His friends to get a move on. He would meet them later on the far shore because, as Mark notes, He wanted to stay behind and pray privately. So, the disciples climbed into a boat and set out while He ascended a mountain nearby in solitude.[5]

The journey should have been quick, only a handful of miles, but the sea refused to behave. A storm blew up once they were out on the water. The winds opposed them so fiercely the disciples made little headway across the lake, even after hours of steady rowing and with several experienced sailors at the helm.

Up on the mountain, Jesus saw the storm roll in too. He looked out where the dark lake stretched below Him, and from His safe and elevated vantage point, He could see His friends were in serious trouble. He knew it was too much for them. Quick as a flash, He climbed down. He left His privileged place in His Father's presence and went after them.

It was all the disciples could do to stay afloat. Sleep deprived and soaked to the bone, they continued to row until well past midnight. Things went from bad to worse. One of them looked up and saw what could only be a ghost striding their way. There in the middle of the raging sea, a phantom figure walked on the waves as if they were made of rock, impervious to the storm and unimpeded by the wind.

Stranger still, as they squinted through the sheets of rain, they noticed this ghost had a face like Jesus. Now they were really terrified.

Right away, a voice shouted out, "Don't be afraid! It's Me! The I Am is with you!" They looked at one another in confusion, because that was unmistakably Jesus's voice.

Here we must hit pause so that the point of this scene is not lost on us. John, who was in the boat that night rowing for dear life, tells us they were more than three miles out to sea when Jesus came into view.[6] I do not know the typical rate of speed for walking on water, but covering this distance on ground would take the better part of an hour. Factor in the intense wind gusts and the rise and fall of the enormous waves, and it is safe to assume Jesus had been walking on the lake for much longer.

If the contrast between God and man wasn't clear enough in the huge catch of fish, it certainly was now. Jesus could do *extraordinary* things, things no other human could hope to do. Not only was He standing on top of liquid water, but He was cruising over vast stretches of it at a steady pace. He didn't need a boat, and He could do by Himself what all the disciples put together could not. His authority and power over this sea and its vicious storm—over death—was absolute. He could not be stopped because it could do nothing to Him.

But all that meant nothing if Jesus kept the power and authority for Himself. He was standing there beside the disciples, yes. But that was little comfort in the face of their imminent drowning. He was standing on a sea that was poised to swallow them. What are we to do with a God who cannot die or does not understand death? We can die, and we do. We are afraid, and for good reason. What comfort are His presence and strength if He stands by while we fail? What good is He to us walking on water when we can no longer row?

God's presence at creation brought life into the world. You and I, the human race God calls His masterpiece, came into life through Him. But it is only a short burst of life we now experience, like a mist that evaporates as quickly as it appears. As James mused, "How do you know what your life will be like tomorrow? Your life is like the morning fog—it's here a little while, then it's gone."[7]

Life is His will for us. Not a moment of it, but an endless eternity of life, and our God *is* that Life. Death is separation from Him, like a branch severed from a tree, and we must understand that it is a stark contradiction to what God has willed and spoken over His world. It is temporary, because God does not change His mind. What He spoke in the beginning is forever the plan. And what does that mean for the tyranny of death? What happens when God steps down into a dead world? Life. God is with us.

There is a glorious answer to James's question. What will life be like tomorrow, if death reigns today? To see it, we must keep our thumb tucked in the New Testament and pivot back several generations. We will return to the Sea of Galilee in just a moment. But long before Peter learned to fish or Jesus learned to walk, there was Moses. He too approached the water's edge with a swarm of Israelites trailing him, not to speak, but to accompany them out into freedom. He was following the Lord's voice like a compass.[8]

God had broken them out of Egypt, and they shook off their chains of slavery. They flew out like birds from a cage into the open wilderness where He took all responsibility to navigate and lead the way. The journey would be a long one, but for the moment, He told Moses to set up camp next to the Red Sea. He had something glorious in mind for this spot.

Almost as soon as the tents were pitched and the campfires lit, the ground began to rattle. A dust cloud rose up and shrouded the horizon. Chariot riders emerged from it, followed by the thunder of horse hooves and battle shouts. The Israelites recognized the insignia glinting in the bright sunlight: Egypt. It was the Egyptian army coming to reclaim them as slaves.

The people panicked, for there was nowhere to run. They cried out to Moses in fear and to God. They were only moments away from a fate worse than death, completely helpless. God had purposely positioned them in a dead end against the seashore.

Moses stood up to quiet the stampede. "Don't be afraid. Stand firm and watch God do his work of salvation for you today. Take a good look at the Egyptians today for you're never going to see them again. God will fight the battle for you."[9]

God answered too: "Get moving!" He said. Prayer time was over.

The Israelites watched as Moses raised his staff over the Red Sea, and the wind began to carve an alley through it in response. The water stacked up like walls on either side of it, framing this hidden path on the seabed. He told the people to cross over on it, and one by one, they escaped to the far shore.

Pharaoh's army could only watch as they fled. Like a traffic cop, God's hand held them in check until the last Israelite foot was safely up on the beach. Then He let them charge in after. None of this was happening by accident. He had already confided to Moses, "I will harden Pharaoh's heart, and he will chase after you. I have planned this in order to display my glory through Pharaoh and his whole army. After this the Egyptians will know that I am the Lord!"[10]

The chariots raced down to the bottom of the sea, making up lost time in pursuit. They sped across at full speed. But before they could come back up, God let go of the lasso holding back the walls of water. The ocean suddenly collapsed. The waves angrily roared back to their usual place, crushing every soldier beneath them.

A stunned silence spread over the beach, followed by wild shouts of praise. All of Israel worshipped at the sight of those turquoise waters, now lying placidly in their bed. The very same sea that had brought the Egyptians death had given them life.

As beautiful as the miracle was, God made it plain where to look for His glory in the midst of it—and it was not in the places we'd assume. It was not the churning sea or the strong winds or even the happy people singing their songs of deliverance. Those were all mere effects of the glory He revealed. His glory lay with Egypt. The glory was under the water, buried under His burst of righteous judgment with the charioteers and their weapons. His glory was bound up in weakness and defeat. The parting of the Red Sea declared how God would rescue His people from slavery to sin and its terrifying sting—death. *He* would die. He personally would charge into the water and let the current drag Him under. By dying, He would free us from it. The sea would forever mean life for us and death for Him. His life would become ours.

To pull it off, the Eternal God needed to undergo a transformation. He had to become as breakable as we are. He needed a body that bruised, a spirit that could be broken, and blood to spill. He could not come to earth as God Almighty. So, at the right time, He set aside His divine privileges and became human. To destroy death, He would taste it firsthand. Hebrews tells us:

> *"Because God's children are human beings—made of flesh and blood—the Son also became flesh and blood. For only as a human being could he die, and only by dying could he break the power of the devil, who had the power of death. Only in this way could he set free all who have lived their lives as slaves to the fear of dying."*[11]

Jesus once pointed back to the fabled life of Jonah as iron-clad proof He would not leave us stranded in the fight against death. He told the religious scholars who so loved to follow Him around, "As Jonah was three days and three nights in the belly of a huge fish, so the Son of Man will be three days and three nights in the heart of the earth."[12] Jonah's wild adventure to the bottom of the sea and back up onto land prophesied His death and resurrection. But even more so, it spoke of His determined solidarity with us in ours. "Because Jonah endured it, I will too," we should hear in His words. "I will not abandon you, even in death, not even in resurrection." His mind was made up.

So strong was His love for us, He did not hesitate to take on flesh and blood to lay Himself down. When Jesus met Peter at the lake that first morning, He was already out in the water. That was why He had come, and the only reason for it. He was not there to beat Peter at his own game as a better fisherman but to invite Peter into real life. He would give Himself up at the cross so that Peter could have life on an extravagant level. All those fish were nothing compared to the abundance Jesus was prepared to dole out.

And that night on the stormy Sea of Galilee, the Son of God was not joy-walking to show off His power. He had been in prayer, one with the Father in heaven, and was deliberately sent down to the disciples and their frightened hearts, leaving footsteps on a lake. Jesus was quick to assure them He was no ghost. Ghosts are not alive. They cannot walk on waves, and they most certainly cannot be crucified to bring redemption to humanity. The Savior of the world had to have a body, for He needed to be killed and raised up again by resurrection.

The Jesus who walked out on the surface of the water was mortal. He wanted all His disciples, including us, to understand that God Almighty was on the sea for this very purpose, and He would not be standing on it for long. Death was coming for Him, but so was resurrection. The Holy Spirit had promised David the sea would not be allowed to keep its grip on the Messiah:

"The ropes of death entangled me;
floods of destruction swept over me.
The grave wrapped its ropes around me;
death laid a trap in my path.
But in my distress I cried out to the LORD;
yes, I prayed to my God for help.
He heard me from his sanctuary;
my cry to him reached his ears.
Then the earth quaked and trembled.
The foundations of the mountains shook;
they quaked because of his anger.
Smoke poured from his nostrils;
fierce flames leaped from his mouth.
Glowing coals blazed forth from him.
He opened the heavens and came down;
dark storm clouds were beneath his feet.
Mounted on a mighty angelic being, he flew,
soaring on the wings of the wind.
He shrouded himself in darkness,
veiling his approach with dark rain clouds.
Thick clouds shielded the brightness around him
and rained down hail and burning coals.
The LORD thundered from heaven;
the voice of the Most High resounded
amid the hail and burning coals.
He shot his arrows and scattered his enemies;
great bolts of lightning flashed, and they were confused.
Then at your command, O LORD,
at the blast of your breath,
the bottom of the sea could be seen,
and the foundations of the earth were laid bare.
He reached down from heaven and rescued me;
he drew me out of deep waters."[13]

Peter heard His voice in the storm and did something wondrously Spirit-filled. He shouted back into the darkness and wind, "Lord, if it's really you, tell me to come to you, walking on the water."[14]

"Yes, join Me!" came Jesus's reply.

The others in the boat watched in disbelief as Peter did the unthinkable. He locked his eyes on Jesus and swung his legs overboard. He took a cautious step toward Him, and then another, and then one more. He glanced down at his feet and all around in awe. Perhaps he even jumped up and down, to test it and make sure he wasn't dreaming. He grinned in amazement. The water held together and remained firm under him, and for a glorious string of moments, Peter was walking too.

He had forgotten all about the storm, but then the winds that didn't faze Jesus suddenly regained Peter's attention. He saw the swells tower like trees overhead. He became conscious of the mad thing he was doing. Fear crept into his heart, and natural law went immediately back to work.

"Save me, Lord!" burst from his lungs as he sank underwater. He didn't yet know it, but they were the three most important words he would ever say.

In the blink of an eye, Jesus, perfectly positioned, caught hold of his outstretched arm. He pulled Peter back up, and for a second miraculous time, Peter stood on the lake like it was paved with stone. He coughed and sputtered, gasping for breath and infinitely grateful for Jesus's steady grip. Jesus had plucked him right up from death, giving him once and for always the upper hand over the sea.

"What will your life be tomorrow?" James asked. Resurrection is the answer. For God's glorious secret all along has been that by raising Jesus, He will raise us too. He is with us.

---

1 This story occurs in Luke 5.
2 This story occurs in Genesis 1.
3 Genesis 1:20 MSG
4 Psalm 69:1–2, 14–15 NLT
5 This story occurs in Matthew 14, John 6, and Mark 6.
6 John 6:19 NLT
7 James 4:14 NLT
8 This story occurs in Exodus 14.
9 Exodus 14:13–14 MSG
10 Exodus 14:4 NLT
11 Hebrews 2:14–15 NLT
12 Matthew 12:40 NIV
13 Psalm 18:4–16 NLT
14 Matthew 14:28 NLT

CHAPTER TWO

In over Our Heads

"All streams flow into the sea,
yet the sea is never full.
To the place the streams come from,
there they return again."

– Ecclesiastes 1:7 NIV

The Sea of Galilee is fed by the waters of the Jordan River, which rises to the north among the mountains of Israel and Lebanon. The river flows into the lake and continues some miles downstream to its terminus at the low-lying, barren basin known as the Dead Sea. The Dead Sea is famously salty, despite the Jordan's continual supply of fresh water, due to the region's extreme altitude and the unrelenting sun. It is like a grave and a desert all in one.

The Dead Sea is stubborn. Its bleak name comes from the water's caustic salinity levels, and deservedly so. No marine life can survive there.

But God told life to fill the seas, and when He gives creation a command, it is always obeyed. He promised Ezekiel a day was coming when another river would flood and overtake the Dead Sea's brine. In a vision, Ezekiel saw fresh water gushing from the Lord's presence:

> *"Measuring as He went, He took me along the stream for 1,750 feet and then led me across. The water was up to my ankles. He*

measured off another 1,750 feet and led me across again. This time the water was up to my knees. After another 1,750 feet, it was up to my waist. Then He measured another 1,750 feet, and the river was too deep to walk across. It was deep enough to swim in, but too deep to walk through.

"He asked me, 'Have you been watching, son of man?'

"Then He said to me, 'This river flows east through the desert into the valley of the Dead Sea. The waters of this stream will make the salty waters of the Dead Sea fresh and pure. There will be swarms of living things wherever the water of this river flows. Fish will abound in the Dead Sea, for its waters will become fresh. Life will flourish wherever this water flows. Fishermen will stand along the shores of the Dead Sea. All the way from En-gedi to En-eglaim, the shores will be covered with nets drying in the sun. Fish of every kind will fill the Dead Sea, just as they fill the Mediterranean.'"[1]

We know straight from Jesus's mouth, and John's exceptional memory, that this powerful imagery refers to the coming of the Holy Spirit. What the Jordan could never do, the Holy Spirit would. Like a surging flash flood, He would arrive with tidal wave force and swallow up death. His work would be perfectly interwoven with Jesus's crucifixion, leading Jesus to cry out passionately to those listening:

"If anyone thirsts, let him come to me and drink. Rivers of living water will brim and spill out of the depths of anyone who believes in me this way, just as the Scripture says."(He said this in regard to the Spirit, whom those who believed in him were about to receive. The Spirit had not yet been given because Jesus had not yet been glorified.)"[2]

Jesus glorified is Jesus *resurrected*. The Spirit can, has, and will make alive anyone who connects themselves to the Risen Christ, as gloriously alive as He made Jesus. God promises the same resurrection life will explode in us until the Dead Sea and its desolate waters are indistinguishable from the Living River's source, Christ Himself.

"Look for the fishermen, Ezekiel," God said. "That's the signal it's starting to happen."

The Jordan River has a storied place in Israel's history. Not only is it the natural artery running north to south between the Sea of Galilee and the Dead Sea, but it also forms a protective border in the east. The very first time the Jewish nation set foot on their promised land it was by crossing the Jordan.

They had followed God's careful lead through the wilderness and arrived at the banks in early spring, when the swollen river was running high and swift. Seasonal rains had flooded the Jordan well past its usual width and depth. No bridge or barge was in sight. But the Lord's directions to their leader Joshua were clear: The people were to cross by walking right through it.[3]

"The Chest of the Covenant will go first," God said to Joshua. "Tell the priests to lift the chest onto their shoulders and step in. As soon as they do, watch! You'll see the river pile up like a haystack and give the people safe passage."

It happened just as God said. The priests carried the chest and its Ten Commandments into the Jordan. The flow shrank back, as if a dam had been placed upstream. What water was left in the river bed rushed onward down its course. Miraculously, just as they had at the Red Sea, the Israelites once again crossed over on dry ground. The priests stayed in place with the chest until everyone was through.

The scene would be repeated a few generations later when two faith giants stood side by side on those same riverbanks. Elijah told his protege Elisha he had God's explicit orders to cross the Jordan. It was heavy with meaning, and they both knew it. Elijah had only a few more moments left on earth. The Holy Spirit had repeatedly informed him his time was nearly up, and young Elisha was not ready to say goodbye. He had barely let the old man out of his sight for weeks, fearing death would snatch Elijah when he wasn't looking.[4]

They arrived at the river together, and true to form, there was no bridge or barge. So, Elijah rolled up the shawl on his shoulders and slung it down hard against the surface of the water. The air echoed with a crack, and the river followed suit. It divided, giving the two prophets a dry path to walk on.

Once they crossed, God sent His angels to fetch Elijah. Elisha watched as they swooped low and placed him in their fiery chariot. He could only cry out in heartache as it drove up and beyond his view into heaven.

In the tumult, the shawl fell from Elijah's hand. It came to rest mournfully at Elisha's feet. He bent over and picked up the last remaining link to his spiritual father.

Clutching it, his mind must have drifted back to the first time he met Elijah. Elisha had been at his parents' home, at work in the field. He was plowing up the soil with a team of oxen. Out of nowhere, the legendary prophet appeared and laid the shawl over Elisha's shoulders. Elisha was totally overwhelmed. It was a signal to leave his old life and come with Elijah as his disciple. Just as Peter dropped his nets, Elisha dropped the reins guiding the oxen and followed.

That very shawl was the one in Elisha's hands. Here at the close of their relationship, God had deliberately left it behind. He wanted Elisha to understand this was where the call had led all along. The call into discipleship is a call to come to the water.

Elisha snapped out of his reverie and stared down at the river. He was here now. He also realized he had a problem. He needed to return to the far side of the Jordan, where his life and ministry were literally waiting. But the river had erased its dry pathway along the bottom. In the time it took for Elijah to ascend to heaven, the waters had flowed back to their usual place.

Frustrated and grieving, Elisha took the shawl and struck the river the same way Elijah had. To no one in particular, he shouted out, "Where is the God of Elijah now?" He knew full well where Elijah was. What mattered now was where his mighty God was. God gave His immediate answer. The river obediently split down the middle and let Elisha back across.

The Lord told Joshua to build a monument so that the Israelites' first crossing would not be forgotten. Twelve stones polished smooth from the incessant current were picked up from the riverbed, right in the middle where the priests had stood. There was one rock to represent each ancestral tribe and commemorate everyone who safely passed through the Jordan.

Israel soon moved on from that place and began its conquest throughout Canaan, but by divine design, the stones remained where they were. For generations, the boulders sat by the river, silently witnessing God's tremendous strength to anyone who trickled by. It was not until John the Baptist, however, that they were understood. It would take his prophetic insight and an unforgettable encounter with Jesus to interpret them.[5]

John, too, was sent to the Jordan by God. Gripped by the Holy Spirit, he spent his days preaching and baptizing the masses in its waters. People of every stripe came forward, the bad, the not so bad, and the terrible alike. He pleaded with them to turn from sin and come into the river, pointing at the ancient rock pile. He said, "Don't just say to each other, 'We're safe, for we are descendants of Abraham.' That means nothing, for I tell you, God can create children of Abraham from these very stones."[6]

His sermons seared their consciences. People responded in droves, confessing sins and charging into the water for baptism, until one day even Jesus was standing there in line among them.

No one else knew who He was yet. Jesus had not started His ministry, and He looked like any other young man. The eccentric and shaggy-haired Baptist was the star here, and all the people's eyes were on him. But John's eyes were transfixed on Jesus, as if the Holy Spirit had flicked on a spotlight over Him.

Things got uncomfortable fast. When it was His turn, Jesus stepped into the water and waded out to where John stood waist-deep. The prophet, who had never before lacked words, froze.

He shook his head and stammered under his breath, "I'm the one who needs to be baptized by You." He knew Jesus was not like the others. He had nothing to repent for. This baptism did not make any sense, and even if it did, who was he to dare touch the Lord?

Jesus was insistent. Repentance had nothing to do with it. This act was about righteousness. "It should be done, for we must carry out all that God requires,"[7] Jesus whispered reassuringly.

At that, John timidly agreed and lowered Jesus down into the stream. When the water broke again and Jesus resurfaced, the most beautiful vision decorated the heavens above Him. John and all those gathered on the bank watched as the Holy Spirit gently descended like a dove and perched on Jesus. And then a voice like thunder shook the air with the proud proclamation, "This is my Son, chosen and marked by my love, delight of my life."[8] Another translation tenderly reads, "With Him I am well pleased."[9]

The monument of river stones recalled God's protection and power over nature, but far more importantly, it shouted to everyone in earshot how He would save His people. The priests had carried the Chest of the Covenant into the Jordan, which contained the tablets inscribed with the Mosaic Law. These literal contours of right and wrong had defied physics and held back the rushing water. Righteousness had protected the people from drowning.

We might be tempted to think, if ever there was a picture of Christ to be found in the Old Testament, surely it would be here. We can look at those priests standing like sentinels and imagine our Good Shepherd leading His flock by stilled waters to green new pastures. But John the Baptist adamantly testifies we look elsewhere. For at the Jordan, he watched as God Made Flesh trudged right into the water among the penitents and allowed Himself to be plunged beneath it. He saw Jesus let go of all He was and sink like a stone to the bottom. He did not see God keep His feet dry. He witnessed death, burial, and resurrection.

Christ's baptism was a hugely important moment. Jesus said it in His own words: He had come to the river that day to fulfill all righteousness, to complete the Mosaic Law down to its most minute regulation. He came to give Himself away in pure love.

For the moment Jesus slipped under the current, His perfect righteousness did too, and death shrank back from it like a shadow fleeing the light. The Jordan's waters that covered him were instantly transformed into ones that gave life. He came back up! Jesus split the waters and under an open heaven took in the first glorious breaths of resurrection air. Right on cue, the Holy Spirit fluttered down to mark Him publicly as the One: God's Beloved, the Source, the Giver, the Resurrection Himself.

It was the Father's promise that by His resurrection, all the other stones littering the river bed would now rise too. That age-old heap of rocks waiting on the bank would at last come back to life. Those who had come to the waters and risked baptism with Jesus would find themselves clean, new, and flooded with the Holy Spirit. Their death would be completely overrun by life.

John the Apostle later reflected on the thousand layers of beauty revealed at Jesus's baptism. Worshipping, he invites us to draw near with him in awe:

"Jesus—the Divine Christ! He experienced a life-giving birth and

a death-killing death. Not only birth from the womb, but baptismal birth of his ministry and sacrificial death. And all the while the Spirit is confirming the truth, the reality of God's presence at Jesus' baptism and crucifixion, bringing those occasions alive for us. A triple testimony: the Spirit, the Baptism, the Crucifixion. And the three in perfect agreement. If we take human testimony at face value, how much more should we be reassured when God gives testimony as he does here, testifying concerning his Son."[10]

It's John's invitation to come to the water and see for ourselves, an invitation he extends at God's enthusiastic behest.

God promised Ezekiel in his vision that something extraordinary would happen at the river. The Holy Spirit would flow, and a curiously ordinary sign would mark that it was underway. Ezekiel was to watch for fishermen at work. They were the proof the new river was present and the sea was turning fresh. Fishers, after all, can only make a catch where life is flourishing.

It was not coincidence that the first four men Jesus called as disciples held this profession. Fishing did not cease for them the day He said to drop nets and follow Him, despite this popular misconception. Quite the opposite: fishing was affirmed, transformed, and wonderfully repurposed in their Master's hands. "From now on you'll be fishing for people!"[11] Jesus had said.

So, we should not be the least bit surprised that Jesus dispatched Peter one afternoon out to the lake.[12] A taxman had come to their house in Capernaum to collect dues, and rather than reaching into His wallet, Jesus gave Peter directions to head to the Sea of Galilee with hook and line and start fishing. "Open the mouth of the first fish you catch, and you will find a large silver coin. Take it and pay the tax for both of us."[13]

Peter told the tax collector he would be back in a few moments and then headed dutifully down to the water. He sat on a sun-bleached dock or some rocky outcrop and patiently waited for a tug on his line. And just as God had said to Ezekiel, soon enough his expert hands reeled in a small fish. He pried open the jaws to remove the hook and found the shiny coin Jesus had spoken of.

It's a charming little miracle, but one that doesn't mean much if we forget Peter was no longer fishing for fish. One sardine pulled from a lake is hardly worth celebrating. One *person* lifted from the waters, however, is. One person raised from the dead is an earth-shaking, hell-defeating, God-glorifying watershed. Jesus had deliberately equipped Peter to catch one fish with a solitary line. Peter did not have a net to gather any more, and there was no need. Jesus promised the first one up from the watery depths would have the exact denomination to cover both their needs.

As Peter idled there, watching the bobber dance on the surface of the lake, he probably wondered why Jesus had chosen such an obscure way to pay a tax. He knew His Master far too well to think any of it was random, but the significance was still hidden. The one fish was Jesus Himself, of course, and the coin was His gleaming righteousness. It would take the coming cross for Peter to understand what Jesus was teaching him.

Peter did not yet know it, but this was why Jesus had been born. This was why the Father had placed Him front and center on the world's stage. John the Baptist was right; He had no sin or reason to repent. Jesus had a sterling record of three straight decades without a slip-up. But God had sent Him to the water to fulfill righteousness, and righteousness is more than just avoiding sin or not breaking commandments. It means fulfilling the true spirit behind them too. It means love, mercy, and generous kindness. It means actively doing good while also doing no harm.

Jesus taught that all the tenets in the Mosaic law and the Prophets could be boiled down to two: unfailing love for God and unrequited love for people. What He really meant was that the Old Testament was more than a long list of impossible demands, though it certainly was that as well; soon enough, everyone would see it was His personal biography. Keeping Himself stain-free was just the prelude. His baptism at the Jordan announced the time had come for Jesus the Son to do each good work God had assigned. To fulfill all righteousness meant outward-facing goodness on a divine scale: loving every neighbor, giving away every penny of His spiritual wealth to the poor around Him until we were the ones perfectly righteous in the Father's eyes. The ministry He'd been given would culminate right back where it began in the water. After all was said and done, He would lay down His life for us as the ultimate act of righteousness. Only then would the law be complete.

Jesus sent Peter out to the Sea of Galilee under this context. A taxman was waiting at their door, but Jesus wanted first to be clear on which of them owed the tax.

"Simon, what do you think? When a king levies taxes, who pays—his children or his subjects? . . . The children get off free, right?"[14]

Peter said yes. That was common sense the world over. No king taxes his own sons, and no king hesitates to slap steep tax burdens on everyone else he rules. Peter would have known too that God's subjects are His creatures—Peter and everyone else formed by God's hand. The Lord requires an accounting of us at the end of our lives of all we have done. He requires righteousness. That all tracked for Peter.

Jesus needed his dear friend to understand that as the Son, He and He alone was fully exempt. But the conditions changed the moment He took on skin and bone and became a man. In joining us, He voluntarily moved from Son to garden variety subject, and the bill fell to Him just the same. Jesus the Man had the same obligation to the High King to pay up.

Paul writes, "When the right time came, God sent his Son, born of a woman, subject to the law. God sent him to buy freedom for us who were slaves to the law, so that he could adopt us as his very own children."[15]

Jesus legally owed a righteous life to the Father. It was a fee that was no easier for Him to pay than anyone else. He had works to accomplish and love to extend until each line of the Mosaic Law had been satisfied. But where every other human had failed to deliver, Jesus would succeed.

That was the real purpose behind His baptism. The Father lifted the curtain to show the watching world not only that Jesus could, but that He gladly would. His offering at the cross would be freely given in holy love. And so, the moment His Son emerged again from the river, the Father beamed with joy. "I'm so pleased with Him!" burst out of heaven. That is the sound of God accepting a sweet-smelling sacrifice that meets His exacting standards. He was breathing the fragrance in slowly, savoring it from His celestial throne.

"Yes, I am well pleased." Take heart that Jesus's righteousness is perfectly sufficient for all our needs. All He asks of us is what He asked of Peter, of Joshua, Elisha, and John: Go down to the water and get going!

Hear the call to a newly converted Paul as your own: "The God of our ancestors has handpicked you to be briefed on his plan of action. You've actually seen the Righteous Innocent and heard him speak. You are to be a key witness to everyone you meet of what you've seen and heard. So what are you waiting for?" The words are for all of us. "Get up and get yourself baptized, scrubbed clean of those sins and personally acquainted with God."[16]

Get on with it!

Come. That is the one call issuing over and over from heaven. "Come to the waters!"[17] He beckons. Come right up and run into the river. Come take a leap and immerse yourself. Don't shy away. Come believing and ready. Come see for yourself how death shrinks back when you dive in and the Spirit is poured out. Come out where it is deep, too deep to touch the bottom any longer. Lose the last foothold and let go. Come take His righteousness. Come where Jesus came and let living waters flow out in you as they do in Him. Come, let Him raise you, and just watch what that unstoppable River does when He enters the sea.

Come. Come be united to Jesus in the water, for that is the purpose of our baptism. He is with us. Now from the river hear Him call out, "Come be with Me!"

---

1 Ezekiel 47:3–6, 8–10 NLT
2 John 7:37–39 MSG
3 This story occurs in Joshua 3–4.
4 This story occurs in 2 Kings 2.
5 This story occurs in Matthew 3, Mark 1, Luke 3, and John 1.
6 Matthew 3:9 NLT
7 Matthew3:15 NLT
8 Matthew 3:16–17 MSG
9 Matthew 3:17 NIV
10 1 John 5:6–9 MSG
11 Luke 5:10 NLT
12 This story occurs in Matthew 17.
13 Matthew 17:27 NLT
14 Matthew 17:25–26 MSG
15 Galatians 4:4–5 NLT
16 Acts 22:14–16 MSG
17 Isaiah 55:1 NIV

CHAPTER THREE

Water to Wine

"And no one pours new wine into old wineskins.
Otherwise, the new wine will burst the skins;
the wine will run out and the wineskins will be ruined.
No, new wine must be poured into new wineskins."

– Luke 5:37–38 NIV

Aaron walked with his brother down to where the Nile met the fertile shoreline, where the reeds grew tall and water was always in supply. The king was already there, to bathe or perhaps to worship the river god, along with his entourage of officials and attendants. Aaron held up a wooden staff for everyone to see. He was an old man, well into his eighties, but he had not brought it to lean on. He lifted it high, raised his other hand, and gave Pharaoh one last warning not to cross God. Then he brought the staff down in a swift stroke on the river. Its sapphire waters instantly thickened and turned red with blood.[1]

Pharaoh had seen the staff before. It was the same one Aaron had thrown down in his throne room and turned into a serpent. The magic trick did little to impress the king, for his own court advisors and jesters easily duplicated the feat. Aaron's serpent swallowed up the others as Pharaoh looked on, and when he grabbed it by the tail, it turned once more into solid wood.

Pharaoh couldn't have cared less. He did not understand what God was saying, nor did he have any desire to listen. But that was a fatal mistake.

For God was speaking about much more than slaves' rights and political muscle. In Aaron's hand was the staff, the ruling stick that kings carried and the rod that shepherds wielded. It was a symbol of the coming Christ. He would be thrown down before the world and crushed underfoot by the devil, but only for a moment. Resurrection would invert the score as God Himself exalted Jesus to the highest throne and greatest glory. The snake would lose and the staff would end up firmly in His hand. It was a triumph God planned to pour out on anyone who trusted in His Christ, anyone who called on Jesus and acknowledged His absolute Lordship. Aaron lifted the staff in one hand and his faith in the other, and the Nile ran red. Liberation was imminent for Israel.

Bible simply means book, but if we were to retitle the Word according to its primary theme, the new name would surely read *The Death of Death*. Scripture abounds with stories that make death's demise at the hand of Jesus quite plain. Read any page and you will see it does not end well for the antagonist, for our hero wields the power of resurrection.

In Genesis, we see how Noah ran out of the Ark after an unthinkably cramped and smelly year inside. The flood that brought judgment receded, and God vowed by the rainbow those waters would never have the power to destroy life on earth again. Like a matchstick, He snapped the sea's only weapon across His knee, and Noah inherited the whole earth.

In Exodus, we see how Moses and the Israelites wandered through the burning desert without water. On the third day, they arrived at an oasis only to find the water there too bitter to drink. God healed it, making the water sweet and turning death's sting into abundant life for His people.

In Kings, we see how Elisha cured poisoned water so it no longer harmed the people or their farmland. God rejected the curse death brought on that place, doubling back destruction on death itself. We also see Elisha raise an axe head from the river bottom, causing iron to miraculously float up on command. Death not only will be defeated, but God promises it will give back everything it has taken from us. He has a record of every loved one, every ache, every grief it owes for. He will strip death bare and return these treasures to us.

Isaiah saw the coming Kingdom where calf and lion could lie side by side, and an infant was perfectly immune to a cobra's venom. Peace gloriously reigned and graced the world. Waters fill the sea for now, God declared, but that ocean will one day yield to the new reality. People brimming with intimate knowledge of their God will move in and upend the water. Death will lose every inch of its ground.

And in Revelation, John saw it had happened. He realized there was something very different about the new landscape God was showing him. Like a field reporter, he scribbled in his notes, "I saw 'a new heaven and a new earth,' for the first heaven and the first earth had passed away, and there was no longer any sea."[2] The sea was completely missing from the picture because death is strictly prohibited in this glorious new realm of creation. God Himself will dwell among His people and be the very light of day. He will be with us, heaven and earth conjoined, for good. You can look, but the sea will never again be there.

Across the Bible, each story rings with resurrection tones and speaks loud and clear of Jesus's decisive victory. Can you see Him Who Lives Again? Can you hear Him? He is the One who boasts of the sea, "I locked it behind barred gates, limiting its shores. I said, 'This far and no farther will you come. Here your proud waves must stop!'"[3]

The sea was gone. What is a world without an ocean? It is a wine cellar.

The first story John transcribes for us in his gospel is the Wedding at Cana, where water became wine and he got a glimpse of Jesus's glory with wide, believing eyes. John himself was much like a good bottle of wine. He burst onto the scene in Mathew, Luke, and Mark as a hotheaded, impulsive, and thunderous young son of a gun. He even bragged to Jesus he deserved to sit beside the Lord when He finally took David's throne. It was arrogant and self-centered, but mostly it was painfully stupid. Taken aback, Jesus told John he had no idea what that request really meant.

"You don't know what you are asking," Jesus said. "Can you drink the cup I drink or be baptized with the baptism I am baptized with?"[4]

John didn't blink. "Yes," he said cockily. Jesus assured him that he would indeed share in all the suffering and death laid out for the Messiah. But places of honor, including His own, were up to the Father to hand out.

Jesus deliberately worked on John more than any other disciple, transforming his immaturity through close fellowship, discipline, and an extravagant dollop of the Holy Spirit. He outlived the other eleven apostles and experienced a lengthy and isolated period of exile. The additional time God granted turned a juice box into a cask of Cabernet Sauvignon. John mellowed and changed qualities so dramatically that by the time he picked up his pen, he had filtered every memory, feeling, and desire through divine love.

His gospel stands in stark contrast to the other three. They tell the stories of Jesus's ministry in full-color narrative; his is a picture book. Written in a child's vocabulary, it is deliberately simple and focused. After decades of meditation and humble friendship with the Holy Spirit, the subtleties of Jesus's words and identity became immensely meaningful. John saw the glory of God again and again in the smallest things His Master had done—how He moved, how He ate, how He responded to people—and wrote a book calling everyone to come behold the brilliant light that is Jesus Christ.

The Wedding at Cana was the rare occasion that required no such incubation period. John tells us he and the disciples saw Jesus's glory right away. Fitting, as the story is about the miracle of instant wine.[5]

They had been invited to the wedding with Jesus and His mother. It was not long into the festivities before the host family ran out of wine, which was both a huge cultural faux pas and the definition of a terrible party. The passage is heavily symbolic by design: Jesus's mother, representing Israel, then came to her Son to alert Him to the trouble. He responded, "Dear woman, that's not our problem. My time has not yet come."[6]

It sounds oddly cold coming from the tenderhearted Jesus we know so well, but again, this is metaphorical speak. The *our* He references is the disciples and Himself. There is a divide between those under the New Covenant with Christ and those under the Old, Israel. The problem the Old Covenant was facing is not one for the New, thank God!

But that problem was a massive one: the Old had no more wine. You can picture Mary pleading with her Son here as every prayer offered from Genesis to Malachi, every sacrifice, every Nazirite fasting in anointed intercession, every desperate plea raised to heaven for God to do something about the threat and reality of death. The wine had run out.

All these prayers were deafening God's ears to send His Messiah, and here at last was Jesus. God had heard their cries. But the time still was not right, for it was the Father's honor to distribute new wine, not the Son's.

Jesus's only part in the miracle was to make it, and that required water. He needed Mary, the disciples, and all of us to understand His death had to come first.

He ordered the wedding servers to fill six enormous jars on hand with water. John clues us in that these were used by the Jews for ceremonial washing. They were little seas, but the glory of God was about to break out over them. Resurrection was brewing.

Jesus told the servers to dip out a taste from the jars for the wedding's Master of Ceremonies. Just one glass, one single life raised up from all those waters, would be presented first to the Lord of all for His approval. As they filled the cup, the servers saw it was no longer clear water but rich, full-bodied wine. The MC was delighted with it! John recalled, "When the host tasted the water that had become wine (he didn't know what had just happened but the servants, of course, knew), he called out to the bridegroom, 'Everybody I know begins with their finest wines and after the guests have had their fill brings in the cheap stuff. But you've saved the best till now!'"[7]

Instantly, the water in the jars was all changed to wine, gallons upon gallons of the very best vintage. John looked around that banquet hall as the new wine was poured and each person in attendance happily raised their cup. That was when the glory hit him full force. Everyone, Old Covenant and New, had it in hand because of Jesus.

John was present when Jesus later taught His disciples that wine is His blood, and whenever we see it in Scripture, we ought to train ourselves to think of salvation. That is what His blood means for us. It brings deliverance and freedom, and its impact on our lives is like the joy of a bottle or two of bubbly shared among lifelong friends. He intends for us to revel in it. To raise a glass is deeply honoring to the Savior and to the Father who sent Him.

Scripture is plain that we should make it our habit to celebrate everything God has done on our behalf. Wine is not reserved for heaven's final curtain call. We ought to drink up every time He works good into our individual lives. He means daily! Every move of His hand flows from that grand salvation and should prompt us to cheerful praise.

The places of honor to Jesus's left and right had already been set for His coronation, just as He told John. He was crucified between a pair of common thieves, and it was His shed blood there that opened the kingdom. The painful cross called to mind a startlingly positive image from Numbers. Long, long before, God had sent scouts into Canaan to reassure the Israelites good things lay ahead for them in the Promised Land. The scouts returned with eye-popping accounts of a land flowing with milk and honey, as well as with a record-breaking cluster of grapes in tow. This one cluster hung on a pole and was so large it took two men to carry it, one on the right and one on the left. God wanted all His people to see it and know they had no reason to be afraid.[8]

Christ looked every bit the part of that bruised cluster on His cross, and we must see Him as God intends. Come look again and you will see the wine is His blood. You will then overflow with joyful gratitude and sing out with all His worshippers:

> *"I love the Lord, for he heard my voice; he heard my cry for mercy. Because he turned his ear to me, I will call on him as long as I live. The cords of death entangled me, the anguish of the grave came over me; I was overcome by distress and sorrow. Then I called on the name of the Lord: 'Lord, save me!' What shall I return to the Lord for all his goodness to me? I will lift up the cup of salvation and call on the name of the Lord."*[9]

The Wedding at Cana harkened back to another much-loved Old Testament story, that of the patriarch Joseph. Joseph was Jacob's favorite son, but we would hardly know it from the constant hatred and opposition he faced at home. His mother died when Joseph was very young, and his many half-brothers were murderously jealous of the extra affection Jacob showered on him in the aftermath. Their hate eventually boiled over into violence. One day they jumped Joseph, threw him in a pit, stripped him bare, and sold him to passing slave traffickers. They covered their tracks by claiming a wild animal had eaten the boy. The lie crushed their father with decades of grief.[10]

The slave traders transported Joseph to Egypt, where they sold him on as chattel to a local official. After some time in this service, trouble reared its ugly head once more for Joseph. He was accused of sexual assault on the job and thrown straight into prison.

The accusations were unfounded, but it made no difference. He sat in the dungeon without hope of release. He was a mere slave after all, a foreigner without friend or family, let alone any legal advocate. But down in that dark, dank cell, he met two fellow prisoners with powerful connections. Both worked in the palace with Pharaoh and held high ranks. Both had managed somehow to irk him and received jail time for their efforts.

The first was Pharaoh's Cupbearer, the man who placed the king's cup in his hand and filled it with wine. Joseph befriended him, and one morning he shared with Joseph a dream he'd had the night before. He said, "In my dream there was a vine in front of me with three branches on it: It budded, blossomed, and the clusters ripened into grapes. I was holding Pharaoh's cup; I took the grapes, squeezed them into Pharaoh's cup, and gave the cup to Pharaoh."[11]

The dream had a relatively straightforward interpretation. "In three days, you'll be back on the job!" Joseph told the Cupbearer.

The other prisoner was Chief Baker to Pharaoh. He was in charge of the bread and baked goods set on Pharaoh's table each day, and he piped up that he also had had a poignant dream. He had seen himself carrying three baskets of bread and pastries, just as he had always done in the palace, but rather than delivering them to the king, birds were helping themselves.

At that, Joseph probably swallowed hard and gave a sideways glance to the Cupbearer. Then he let it rip: "This is the interpretation: The three baskets are three days; within three days Pharaoh will take off your head, impale you on a post, and the birds will pick your bones clean."[12] It was not exactly the encouragement the Baker was hoping for.

The Holy Spirit had seized the moment to speak frankly about the crucifixion. Broken bread. Wine poured out and then generously refilled. A grisly death, pierced on a wooden beam. Reunion after three days.

Things played out exactly as Joseph had said. That same week, the Baker was executed and the Cupbearer was restored to his position in the king's presence. And though he had asked the Cupbearer to put in a good word for him, poor Joseph was utterly forgotten. The Cupbearer left the dungeon and did not look back.

The million-dollar question we must ask is what the foreshadowed cross had to do with Joseph's miserable conditions. Or rather, what good was it to Joseph? Why did the Holy Spirit bother to bring it up? Scripture tells us he spent two more years locked up in that underground cell living anything but what could genuinely be called a life. It was more like waiting in a mausoleum, waiting to be pulled back up into the real world.

The day finally came when God stirred Pharaoh's heart to send for Joseph. He too had had mysterious dreams and needed a reliable interpreter, and the Cupbearer suddenly remembered the slave he had met down in the prison. In a flash, Joseph was plucked from squalor and seated in honor beside Pharaoh. That is resurrection, and it is beautifully redemptive.

But what of those long, lonely, unjust years Joseph had no choice but to endure? What took so long? Joseph was a good man who lived fairly and walked in lockstep with the Holy Spirit. He did not deserve what he suffered. He was wise, but catastrophe found him anyway. He knew both God and what God planned to do. He knew resurrection was coming for Israel and asked on his deathbed for his bones to go with Moses into Canaan. He even understood that God's immediate plans were really speaking about eternal ones, for "the essence of prophecy is to give a clear witness for Jesus,"[13] always. His whole life shimmered with hints of Jesus's future mistreatment and glory and is of course inspirational to study for that very reason. Yet he waited like a dead man in his tomb.

The answer lies with the Cupbearer. He needed to come to his position first in order to intercede for Joseph. When God was ready and the time was right, the Cupbearer was standing beside the king. The cup of wine was in Pharaoh's hand, and Joseph's name came from the Cupbearer's mouth. It is the Father, remember, who distributes the wine because the Son provided it.

This is precisely the message Peter preached to the crowd gathered on the Day of Pentecost.[14] First Christ crucified, then Christ resurrected; and to complete His glorious saving work, Christ ascended:

> *"People of Israel, listen! God publicly endorsed Jesus the Nazarene by doing powerful miracles, wonders, and signs through him, as you well know. But God knew what would happen, and his prearranged plan was carried out when Jesus was betrayed. With the help of lawless Gentiles, you nailed him to a cross and killed him. But God released him from the horrors of death and raised him back to life, for death could not keep him in its grip... God raised Jesus from the dead, and we are all witnesses of this. Now he is exalted to the place of highest honor in heaven, at God's right hand. And the Father, as he had promised, gave him the Holy Spirit to pour out upon us, just as you see and hear today... So let everyone in Israel know for certain that God has made this Jesus, whom you crucified,*

to be both Lord and Messiah!"[15]

Forty days after Easter, the disciples witnessed Jesus taken up into heaven. He vanished before their eyes into the clear blue sky. They sat around for ten more days, wondering what on earth came next. The Holy Spirit was the answer to that. He came right on cue on the morning of Pentecost, not announcing some new phase but as a heavenly sign the one and only plan was complete. Jesus was now on His high throne, beyond the reach of death and grave forever and seated beside the Father in honor.

The Spirit came like a rushing wind on the disciples, but His effect was like wine. The first glass had been dipped out and taken up to the Master of Ceremonies. The Father had given His full stamp of approval to the Son, and now the rest of the batch was ready. Onlookers joked that the baby church staggered and babbled like drunks under the Spirit's influence. Not that they minded; not in the least. Life had become a party through salvation.

> *"And all the believers met together in one place and shared everything they had. They sold their property and possessions and shared the money with those in need. They worshipped together at the Temple each day, met in homes for the Lord's Supper, and shared their meals with great joy and generosity—all the while praising God and enjoying the goodwill of all the people. And each day the Lord added to their fellowship those who were being saved."*[16]

Scripture is completely tight-lipped on what happened in heaven those first ten days Jesus was back home, but we should take heart that God did not forget His dear ones waiting patiently through them. Jesus was inaugurated and the Spirit came. Always trust He will remember and send fresh help when it is most needed. There will always be new wine in your cup to raise in gracious response. His Spirit dwells with us until the very end and will resupply encouragement, wisdom, strength, and power. That is what the story of Joseph ultimately proclaims.

Proverbs reminds us wine is a gift to those who languish, because the wait can often be long and the trouble we encounter can be overwhelming. And while death may no longer be fatal for the Church, God knows it is still a daily problem. We do not face it alone:

> *"It is not for kings, O Lemuel, to guzzle wine. Rulers should not crave alcohol. For if they drink, they may forget the law and not give justice to the oppressed. Alcohol is for the dying, and wine for those in bitter distress. Let them drink to forget their poverty and remember their troubles no more. Speak up for those who cannot speak for themselves; ensure justice for those being crushed. Yes, speak up for the poor and helpless, and see that they get justice."*[17]

Hear what Scripture is saying. Jesus's exalted position beside the Father is good news for us who feel abandoned and oppressed. We are waiting for the day when death is finally gone and we share the glorious bodily resurrection Jesus experienced. We groan as we wait for His coming and His justice! Christ has not forgotten us in paradise but is in His God-arranged position to intercede on our behalf even now. Whenever your weary head droops and your spirit feels faint, have confidence wine is on its way. He has ascended for this very purpose.

There is a day on the Lord's calendar when death does indeed expire, scheduled in permanent marker long before the world began. That is the day when resurrection wildfire breaks out on the earth and everyone connected to Jesus comes alive at once. The cups of wine along the way are God's gift to help us endure. He provides little tastes of resurrection to assure He will see it through. The end will come like a net cast into the deep sea, drawing up every fish from the water. Tombs will be vacated, breath breathed back into dry bones. Death will be emptied, shamed, and finally abolished for good. It will become a nonsense word no one speaks anymore. Resurrection will have replaced it.

Paul lays it all out in 1 Corinthians:

> *"Christ has been raised from the dead. He is the first of a great harvest of all who have died. So you see, just as death came into the world through a man, now the resurrection from the dead has begun through another man. Just as everyone dies because we all belong to Adam, everyone who belongs to Christ will be given new life. But there is an order to this resurrection: Christ was raised as the first of the harvest; then all who belong to Christ will be raised*

> *when he comes back. After that the end will come, when he will turn the Kingdom over to God the Father, having destroyed every ruler and authority and power. For Christ must reign until he humbles all his enemies beneath his feet. And the last enemy to be destroyed is death."*[18]

That is what our Jesus is doing now, reigning. God is strategically and systematically bringing every rebellious spiritual power under His Lordship until death shrivels up in defeat. Every act of His Spirit, every good deed, every time the Church advances and His children experience grace, Christ's reign strengthens and our confidence in Him grows. It will not be much longer.

Why are we so certain? Because of His continued goodness. Because of the Spirit's presence as a deposit within us guaranteeing full resurrection. Because of the moments where the clouds break and we see His face clearly. Yes, for all these reasons, but only because they are rooted in the truth of Jesus. His grave is vacant because He is alive. That is where our true confidence rests.

The Savior is not sitting around in heaven twiddling His thumbs. We can trust Him to save us and trust that His salvation is already underway. Paul paints the picture of an aggressive, active attack on death's borders. Close your eyes and you can see Christ like Julius Caesar at the battle front. His sword and scepter are raised. The cry has sounded for His forces to advance. Watch death tremble behind those fortress walls. It knows the end brings total annihilation.

If you have ever wondered what His death means for your life, wonder no more. Mark contains a drama for the ages to put everything in perspective. One afternoon Jesus and His disciples set out to cross the Sea of Galilee. The weather was beautiful, so Jesus took advantage of the fair skies and sublime conditions. He retreated to the back of the boat, curled up on a cushion, and promptly fell asleep, leaving the short sail in His disciples' capable hands. But not long after He lay down, rough winds rose from nowhere and a storm whipped up the water. Huge waves threatened to fill the boat.[19]

One of the men shook Jesus awake, in total disbelief He could be sleeping at a time like this. He shouted, "Teacher, don't you care that we're going to drown?"[20]

Jesus jumped to His feet and gave the storm a stinging rebuke to be still. Instantly, the waters settled down and the clouds became silent, almost ashamed of themselves. They recognized their Master.

The disciples were completely dumbstruck. They looked at one another and could only ask, "Who is this man? Even the winds and waves obey him!"[21]

They saw a man but realized they were also seeing God, God in all His fullness who was pleased to dwell in Jesus. They saw Christ, who was asleep in death, raised and reascended to His divine throne. They saw Him wield His power and absolute authority over the sea. They saw Him personally overcome death.

But the revelation was far from over. Their heads were still spinning as the boat completed the crossing. They landed on the outskirts of a town named Gerasa. It seemed like a decent place to dock, and they proceeded to tie up and disembark. With a shudder, however, they quickly realized they had arrived on the grounds of a cemetery.[22]

As if that wasn't uncomfortable enough, a mad man suddenly came tearing from his hiding place among the tombs straight at Jesus. He was filthy and naked except for his scraggly, unkempt hair. He was covered in cuts and scars. He often slashed his arms and legs, using rocks like blades against himself. No one could subdue him or even keep him bound in a chain.

He bellowed and screamed like a wounded animal, out for blood, but mysteriously stopped short. He collapsed at Jesus's feet in an awkward bow and began to plead for mercy, begging Jesus to get back in the boat and leave the area.

He was a dead man walking. The whole place reeked of death. Many, many demons possessed him, locking him up like a prisoner of war among the gravestones. But Jesus stood like a pillar and did not flinch. He was not intimidated, nor even surprised at what He witnessed.

"Out of him!" He commanded.

Call to mind again the image of Julius Caesar leading the charge, for Scripture wants us to understand Jesus had crossed the Rubicon by the time He reached Lake Galilee's far shore. He had crushed the sea and now set His pierced feet on Gerasa's graveyard. It immediately became holy ground. Oh, what a fool the devil was to think death would destroy Jesus. All it did was let Him walk in through hell's front door, and He had not come to play nice. He declared:

> *"If I am casting out demons by the Spirit of God, then the Kingdom of God has arrived among you. For who is powerful enough to enter the house of a strong man and plunder his goods? Only someone even stronger—someone who could tie him up and then plunder his house."*[23]

Jesus's footsteps on the beach of Gerasa rattled the ground with seismic tremors. The thousands of evil spirits haunting it saw Him instantly. What was the Lord of heaven and earth, the Eternal Living God, doing *inside* death's gates? That was what sent the madman barreling toward Him. They knew His superior power was uncomfortably close. They could feel their stronghold dissolving all around them.

Jesus stood there in all His glory. Hear the Psalms' refrain like a herald's trumpet blast:

> *"The earth is the Lord's, and everything in it.*
> *The world and all its people belong to him.*
> *For he laid the earth's foundation on the seas*
> *and built it on the ocean depths.*
> *Open up, ancient gates!*
> *Open up, ancient doors,*
> *and let the King of glory enter.*
> *Who is the King of glory?*
> *The Lord, strong and mighty;*
> *the Lord, invincible in battle."*[24]

"Out of him!" Jesus said.

Time was up. His victory over death meant victory for everyone else it terrorized. The legion of dark forces fled, and the man was wholly free.

He had not moved an inch, yet Jesus had invaded and reclaimed death's territory as His own. He flooded death with life and removed every foul trace of Satan's former kingdom. Scripture tells us the man put on clothes and sat right down at Jesus's feet, fully sane and calm. He was able to speak like a human. He went back into the city to reconnect with his family members. He traveled all through the region telling everyone he could find of the incredible kindness Jesus had shown him. Who can guess how long he had missed human company and warmth! How long he had been dead! God gave him everything back in Christ.

Why are we so confident? Because Jesus lives, and nothing can change that. We never need to fear the sea again, no matter how it froths or rises. We know those waters will turn to wine soon enough.

We can face them with courage like Paul. On his final mission journey into Rome, he experienced utter disaster. The weather did not cooperate, the boat would not stay on course, and delays forced the crew to risk sailing in the tumultuous autumn and winter months. The gamble backfired, and Acts recounts the harrowing weeks he and the other passengers spent battling a typhoon on the Mediterranean Sea. They could not find ports or control the ship in the furious gales. They lost all commercial cargo the ship was carrying and had to sacrifice every life boat and anchor to keep afloat. Conditions were so severe that days and nights went by without anyone even eating. This is often what life with Christ is like, and there is no use pretending otherwise. Trouble will always come, and Paul was not surprised by it.[25]

But at last, when things were at their bleakest, the wine appeared. God sent word in the night to encourage Paul, who shared His message with everyone on board:

> *"Men, you should have listened to me in the first place and not left Crete. You would have avoided all this damage and loss. But take courage! None of you will lose your lives, even though the ship will go down. For last night an angel of the God to whom I belong and whom I serve stood beside me, and he said, 'Don't be afraid, Paul, for you will surely stand trial before Caesar! What's more, God in his goodness has granted safety to everyone sailing with you.' But we will be shipwrecked on an island."*[26]

Those listening probably did not find the same level of comfort Paul did hearing shipwreck was inevitable. But that was because they did not yet understand what God meant. A few days later, the ship did indeed break apart and sink off the coast of Malta. They bottomed out in a shallow bay, and the boat was smashed to pieces by the rough waves. It was a total loss, but true to God's word, everyone was able to grab hold of the debris and swim to shore safely.

Common sense says to jump when you know the ship is going down. Paul, however, was adamant no one left before it sank, including the pagan crew. "[He] said to the centurion and the soldiers, 'Unless these men stay with the ship, you cannot be saved.'"[27] Their lives, and the fulfillment of God's promise to protect them, depended on it. Into the sea they all went.

Not one person drowned. The wreck that now lay under the surf had provided their escape from it. They emerged on the beach and held high, like a champagne flute, the bits of wood that had saved their lives.

1 This story occurs in Exodus 7.
2 Revelation 21:1 NIV
3 Job 38:10–11 NLT
4 Mark 10:38 NIV
5 This story occurs in John 2.
6 John 2:4 NLT
7 John 2:9–10 MSG
8 This story occurs in Numbers 13.
9 Psalms 116:1–4, 12–13 NIV
10 This story occurs in Genesis 37, 39–41.
11 Genesis 40:9–11 MSG
12 Genesis 40:18–19 MSG
13 Revelation 19:10 NLT
14 This story occurs in Acts 2.
15 Acts of the Apostles 2:22–24, 32–33, 36 NLT
16 Acts of the Apostles 2:44–47 NLT
17 Proverbs 31:4–9 NLT
18 1 Corinthians 15:20–26 NLT
19 This story occurs in Mark 4, Matthew 8, and Luke 8.
20 Mark 4:38 NLT
21 Mark 4:41 NLT
22 This story occurs in Mark 5, Matthew 8, and Luke 8.
23 Matthew 12:28–29 NLT
24 Psalms 24:1–2, 7–8 NLT
25 This story occurs in Acts 27.
26 Acts of the Apostles 27:21–24, 26 NLT
27 Acts 27:30–31 NIV

Picture Two: *Ground*

CHAPTER FOUR

Written In the Dirt

"The Word became flesh and made his dwelling among us. We have seen his glory, the glory of the one and only Son, who came from the Father, full of grace and truth."

–John 1:14 NIV

"Samuel!"

The little boy turned over on his mat, roused by the sound of his name. It was dark inside the tent, and the lamplight softly flickered off to one side. He rubbed the sleep from his eyes and jumped to his feet.[1]

He ran out to the priests' quarters, right up to Eli's bedside. The old man was sound asleep. Everyone was. Samuel shook him awake.

"You called for me, sir. I'm here!" Samuel whispered.

Eli stared at him blankly, trying to understand what was happening. He was puzzled the boy was in front of him.

"What are you doing up? I didn't call you. Get back in bed," he growled. He lay back down and waved Samuel off.

Samuel ran back to his mat as he was told, but no sooner had he stretched out than he heard it again.

"Samuel! Samuel!" He returned to Eli.

"Here I am!" he said, panting a little. Eli was not amused.

"I told you to go to bed. No more of this—lie down and sleep."

It happened a third time. "Samuel!" When the boy appeared by his bed once more, Eli realized Samuel wasn't playing games. He really was hearing something, and that something was God's holy, still, small voice in the quiet of the Tabernacle. Samuel's sleeping mat was on the ground just across from the Chest of the Covenant, where God was enthroned. Eli realized it was the Lord calling out his name.

"Go back and wait on your mat. If you hear it again, stay where you are and listen closely."

Samuel was in the right place at very much the wrong time. It had been decades since God had spoken to anyone like this, Eli included, and Israel had grown unresponsive and spiritually dim. Israel had become like an animal that lives underground and has lost the use of its eyes. A metaphor for the whole nation, head priest Eli too was old, feeble, ineffective, and nearly blind. However, though no one was looking for it, Scripture tells us the lamp of God had not burned out. There was still light in the Tabernacle, for God had not abandoned His beloved people nor given up His purpose. He was still right there.

"Samuel!" came a fourth time. Eli had told him how to respond to God's Spirit. So, from his humble bedroll, Samuel answered, "Speak, Lord. I'm listening."

Samuel's first encounter with the Lord was not his last. He grew up as a tried and true prophet from that point forward. He relayed messages from God to His people and lifted their prayers in return to God's throne. His appointment to intercessory work was very similar to what Moses experienced a few generations earlier.

Moses, too, had been in the right place at seemingly the wrong time. He was a shepherd overseeing his father-in-law's flock, a line of work he came into completely by accident. Born and raised in Egypt, Moses fled for the border after murdering a man. Over the next forty years, he built a new life for himself in the land of Midian and put the past behind him. He married a local man's daughter after her family offered him hospitality, and in exchange, he helped keep the sheep. He had not set foot in Egypt again for fear of being arrested.[2]

One day, he decided to lead the sheep into the wider wilderness. As he approached the mountains rimming the desert horizon, a strange sight caught his eye. He saw flames burning. A lowly shrub was on fire, which was not an unusual thing to see in that arid climate, but it was not burning up. The fire continued and the bush was unharmed. Moses stared at it in wonder.

"Moses!" a voice suddenly called out from the fire.

"Yes?" he answered in surprise.

"Don't come any closer!" the voice warned. "This is holy ground you are standing on, so take the sandals off your feet."

Moses looked down at his shoes and the dry soil beneath them. Surely, he was perplexed by this command. Holy things are dangerous and off-limits, particularly so when there is murder on your rap sheet. He had no problem standing back from the mystical fire, but going barefoot would remove the thin barrier between him and the holiness he was standing on. Losing his sandals would mean coming into direct contact with it.

But there was no time to argue. The voice continued, "I am the God of Abraham, Isaac, and Jacob, the God your fathers all worshipped." Moses immediately covered his face in fear. He had nowhere to hide, and nowhere to run. Even the very ground was radiating God's presence. He had been found out. Justice had finally caught up with him.

How on earth had he ended up here? He couldn't open his eyes. Yet a moment passed, and he realized God had not struck him down in judgment—nor did it seem like He was going to.

"My name, Moses, is I AM. That is My eternal name, which all generations will call Me," God said gently.

That was what the fiery bush was illustrating, I AM. This little bush was somehow living despite the flames that should have consumed it. It was wrapped in fire and living defiantly on. An eternal name, an eternal existence for the God of his ancestors. And somehow, he, Moses, a sinful man, was able to draw into His intimate company. He knew the stories about this God who had formed the universe and controlled the earth and skies with perfect righteousness. Yet in this moment, it almost felt like He was a friend and the holy ground around the bush was a safe place to stand.

"I have come down to rescue My people, Moses," God said. "You're going to be part of it."

How was it that a fugitive with blood on his hands could partner with God? How could Samuel, a mere child, and one who was neither a priest nor had any prior relationship with the Lord to boot, sleep in peace on the floor before the Ark? The single most dangerous place on the planet was the inner portion of the Tabernacle. Only a curtain separated Samuel from it.

The answer was that God Himself had made it safe. The burning bush was a sign of God's arrival at ground level. The lamp continued to burn in the Tabernacle, a sign of the Lord's presence on Samuel's side of the curtain. God was making a bold declaration that He was here on our turf for our own good.

The apostle John opens his titanic gospel with thunder:

> *"In the beginning was the Word, and the Word was with God, and the Word was God. He was with God in the beginning. Through him all things were made; without him nothing was made that has been made. In him was life, and that life was the light of all mankind. The light shines in the darkness, and the darkness has not overcome it."*[3]

The ever-burning Light, the ever-living Life: John tells us right away this is Jesus. All those years in the Tabernacle, when the lampstand shined through the dark night watches, Jesus was present. What Moses witnessed in the brushfire was Jesus, the almighty I AM sent to walk on earth. As His resurrection would soundly prove, He is a Light that cannot be extinguished and a Life that tramples over death. And He came to earth to help.

John calls Him the Word and tells us He was there for the world's first moment. The Word was already on the scene when creation got underway. In fact, the world owes its very existence to Jesus and continues to exist because of Him.

John 1 is the apostle's annotated creation account, which Genesis 1 describes this way: On day three, a command from the Lord sent the sea running in full retreat. "Land, appear!" He called out. The waters pooled in one corner, submissive to His voice, and dry ground emerged from beneath the waves. Bedrock appeared by His Word, and how His heart must have rejoiced to see it!

With His Word, the Creator transformed the landscape from a blank canvas to an oil masterpiece. Things had existed on days one and two, but it was not until the third day that life began to flow. This was radically new. "Yes, green up, world!" He said. "Leaf out! Bud! Blossom!" He had already decided it would be this way. Plants of every kind would cover the ground, drawing life up from the soil.

In the plans only God foreknew, incredible things lay ahead for that bare clay and granite. He would paint the slopes and valleys a verdant green. The humble ground would hold tree roots and hidden springs, vineyards and jungles and mountain ranges. He would use the clods of dirt to form an endless variety of animals and, most precious of all to His heart, people bearing His own image. The ground would be the backdrop for all of history.

He gripped His palette and set to work. We know, like John, what was happening. The Father was unveiling His blueprint for salvation in these early hours of the creation week. It was day three. Resurrection was woven into the very fabric of the universe from the beginning.

God possesses a divine license that He is fiercely passionate about. The Word was first. He does not ask for permission before He acts, nor does He need anyone's help. He is more ancient than the world, and it exists simply because He told it to do so. He does not wait for someone to reach out for help before He responds. He has His own calculus to determine the right time to move His hand, and it is not based on any clock or merit scale humans can discern. This sheer wildness in His nature is at the very heart of who He is, and the actions that spring from it are called *grace*. Grace is God unleashed, God unprompted, and God at His most unexpected.

The sea did not ask for land. Nor did darkness ask for light at creation, nor did the waters ask for heavenly skies. They exist solely because of grace. God spoke each into being because He wanted them. He had greatness in mind for them, a tremendous desire to show mercy after mercy throughout the millennia ahead.

In Scripture, grace is pictured by the *ground*. The ground is firm, solid, and lasting, established by the eternal Word of God. It is where life flourishes and the oceans cannot advance. It is where God met Moses and where He spoke to Samuel, and it is where He is present and powerfully active through His Son.

Grace looks like many things to the writers of the Bible, such as a welcome place to rest in times of turmoil: "He lifted me out of the pit of despair, out of the mud and the mire. He set my feet on solid ground and steadied me as I walked along."[4]

Or wise guidance to navigate complete confusion: "Teach me to do your will, for you are my God; may your good Spirit lead me on level ground. For your name's sake, Lord, preserve my life; in your righteousness, bring me out of trouble."[5]

Or a pure gift, like an undeserved and unexplainable inheritance that suddenly turns up on the doorstep: "Put your hope in the Lord. Travel steadily along his path. He will honor you by giving you the land. You will see the wicked destroyed."[6]

It all happens because God decided beforehand what He wants to do. Grace flows from His heart out ahead of us, and just like the ground, is set beneath our feet in preparation for us to one day walk on.

Why did God cross paths with Moses that day at Sinai? Why did He place the burning bush right where Moses was leading his sheep? He had already promised Abraham four hundred years earlier that He would. He had given His Word He would not leave Israel in slavery forever. The Word had already gone out ahead of Moses and laid the holy ground in anticipation.

Why did He meet Samuel in the Tabernacle? It was God who came up with the Tabernacle, calling it the Tent of Meeting. He had Moses set it up so there would be a place God could meet His people to talk. Samuel was not seeking God that night, but God was ready to meet him anyway. Grace was at work.

Grace ought to make us drop to our knees in worship, because it exposes how precarious our tiny lives truly are. Absolutely everything hinges on God's grace, on His desire to be kind and generous and faithful toward us. If He were ever to change His mind, we could not argue with Him, or worse, if He were to treat us as we deserve, we would not live to tell the tale.

There was a frightful moment in Moses's history when God did reconsider His plans. Literally everything hung in the balance. Salvation, humanity, the sun ever rising again, the world and the galaxies were all within a hair's breadth of annihilation. Moses could do nothing but step back and watch as God pondered what He wanted to do.

It happened only a few days after Moses led the people through the Red Sea and into the desert. God summoned him to climb Mt. Sinai, the same peak where he had seen the bush, to receive the regulations we know today as the Ten Commandments. Scripture calls them the Law. They comprised a binding covenant between God and His people of how they would behave toward Him. He had invited them into this holy relationship and promised to bless or discipline them in accordance with their actions. God gave Moses additional instructions as well while he was on the summit, such as the construction plan for the Tabernacle and the system of sacrificial sin offerings.[7]

Moses had not even started his descent before God exploded in anger:

> *"Go! Get down there! Your people whom you brought up from the land of Egypt have fallen to pieces. In no time at all they've turned away from the way I commanded them: They made a molten calf and worshipped it. They've sacrificed to it and said, 'These are the gods, O Israel, that brought you up from the land of Egypt! . . . I look at this people—oh! what a stubborn, hard-headed people! Let me alone now, give my anger free reign to burst into flames and incinerate them. But I'll make a great nation out of you."*[8]

It was a terrifying turn of events. Moses was carrying the tablets God's own hand had inscribed with the terms of the Covenant, and he rushed back down to the base of the mountain. As he did, the sound of drumbeats and shouts filled his ears. The people were partying in his absence, convinced he was dead and God was no longer interested in them. Just as God had told him, they had made an idol and were worshipping it with drunken revelry.

Moses could not believe his eyes. He threw the Covenant tablets to the ground and smashed them, for that was what had happened: the people had broken the deal with God just seconds after it was put in place. They were like a bride cheating at the altar, and their unfaithfulness had ignited God's hot fury.

This sin severed the agreement between God and His people. No longer was He bound to bless them or lead them into their new spacious homeland. They had made God an enemy and were on the brink of death.

Moses turned around and pleaded with the Lord not to destroy Israel. The people sobered up fast, realizing they had made a colossal mistake. But it was all up to God, whether He would show mercy or strike them down as they deserved.

Moses waited. It must have been unbearable. At last, the Lord spoke and gave His verdict. "I will indeed take you to Canaan. Yes, you are going to see the glory of God on an exponential level.

"I'm going to show My people more grace than you can fathom, Moses. You'll see all my goodness because of this, because I decide when I show mercy and who I pour it on. Now you're going to understand who I AM. The plan is unchanged."

He told Moses to stand on a rock nearby and to watch. God was about to reveal Himself in breathtaking fashion. The rock He pointed to was split with a deep crack, resembling the broken stone tablets inscribed with the Commandments. God told Moses to hide in that crevice, for Moses needed mercy as much as the people did. He had not joined in the idolatrous affair, but murder was just as prohibited in the Covenant. They had all sinned.

"Look up, Moses," God said. "I'll cover you with My hand as I pass by. You don't understand it now, you can't, but this is My Son. He will protect you in the midst of My holiness, for My heart burns to be close, not to destroy. This Covenant will still hold, for under it is the holy ground He makes safe for you. When you look, you'll see my back, Moses. It means I'm leading you. Trust that, and keep following. And one day, you'll truly see the Living God, the Resurrection, face to face. You'll know then it was the Son, the glory of God, with you all along."

God has spoken, and His Word on the matter is grace. Rest assured in your bleakest moment of insecurity that God will not change His mind. He had the opportunity to scrap the whole plan and do away with His redemptive work. He gave it serious consideration, and it only intensified His desire to care for us. No sin, even the most disgusting ones we can imagine, will ever surprise Him or cause Him to walk off from us. Our future rests safely in His permanent decision to show us continual mercy. Never has it been up to us to deserve it.

Lest we doubt Him, God backed up His promise to Moses with an emphatic public declaration. Many, many years later, Jesus came to the temple one morning to teach. John, who recorded the event for us, deliberately did not include what Jesus was saying. Instead, he detailed what Jesus did. We first see Him sitting, then standing to His feet, and then crouching low in the dirt, only to rise up and bend down again. Up and down, up and down He goes.[9]

Some scholars of the Law brought in a woman. They led her to Jesus and made her stand before Him like a courtroom exhibit. The crowd formed a ring around her, watching intently.

"Teacher," the scholars began, "this woman is an adulteress. She was caught in bed with a man who is not her husband." In their hands were rocks. They had brought her there to stone her for her sin.

John does not describe her, but we can guess that terror was etched on her face. Everyone gathered there knew the penalty for infidelity was death, and there were eyewitnesses to what she had done. Whether she was remorseful over the affair, we do not know. We know nothing about what led to it, how long it lasted, or even how it was found out. John gives us no context or technicalities, and that is precisely the point: all we know, same as the watching crowd did, is that sin definitely occurred. It was a very clear-cut legal case.

The Pharisees asked Jesus, "Should we stone her? That is what the Law of Moses demands. What do You say?"

But Jesus didn't reply. Strangely, He stooped down to the dirt and began to write on the ground with His finger as if He did not hear them. The others were incredulous. They repeated the accusation against her again and again and pushed Him for a decision.

Finally, He stood up. He spoke and then dropped once more to the ground to resume His scribbling on the Temple floor.

The Word, John reminds us, was there in the beginning. He came from heaven, appeared in flesh, and made His dwelling among us. It was the grace of God that brought His Incarnation, and grace was what He came to give out. Up, then down, He came, in the name of grace.

They were seeing it in real time. The Word had descended to the dirt to deal with sin once and for all, but not through the condemnation everyone expected. Something else was at work. Written right there on the ground was Jesus, and that was the Father's final decision.

"All right," Jesus said at last. "Throw the stones at her. Let the one among you who has never sinned go first." He bent down once more.

Rocks began to pound the ground. The woman braced for the worst, but none of them were aimed at her. One by one, they slipped from her accusers' hands and fell into the dirt. The crowd of onlookers melted away without so much as another syllable. Soon only Jesus was left there with her.

Jesus stood up and asked her, "Woman, where did they all go? Is no one going to condemn you?"

"No one's left," she said in shock.

"I'm not condemning you either. Go your way now, and don't sin anymore." Off she walked on solid ground.

---

1 This story occurs in 1 Samuel 3.
2 This story occurs in Exodus 2–4.
3 John 1:1–5 NIV
4 Psalm 40:2 NLT
5 Psalm 143:10–11 NIV
6 Psalm 37:34 NLT
7 This story occurs in Exodus 32.
8 Exodus 32:7–10 MSG
9 This story occurs in John 8.

CHAPTER FIVE

Nothing Is Impossible

"But God's not finished. He's waiting around to be gracious to you.
He's gathering strength to show mercy to you.
God takes the time to do everything right—everything.
Those who wait around for him are the lucky ones."

– Isaiah 30:18 MSG

John lets the story of the adulterous woman end with a cliffhanger. Was she grateful for His mercy? Did she run right back and resume her affair? Did her accusers pursue her again? Did Jesus's intervention only anger them further or did it soften their hearts? Scripture does not say.

That is God's preferred way of working. Grace is maddeningly open-ended. God extends it when He chooses, oftentimes when it genuinely makes no sense to do so, and then leaves it entirely up to us how we will respond.

God did not base His decision to send Christ on anything good He saw in humanity. He did not forgive the adulterous woman because of her tears or because she had reason to leave her husband. He did it because He wanted to. He then put the ball back in her court. She was free to accept the mercy and continue walking with Him—or not. She was free to abuse the grace and blatantly sin again—or not.

We are all free to accept or reject it, and most amazingly of all, God does not factor our response to His grace into His initial decision to extend it. Of course, He knows beforehand what we will do with it. He knows some of us will walk right out of the room and burn Him. He knows full well even the most genuinely grateful among us will fail Him again soon enough. He knows we often need more grace before we can begin to believe. None of it fazes Him. He has decided to offer us grace, independent of any other rationale. It is what makes Him unequivocally good and totally uncontrollable. It's what makes Him God.

Our God delights in being gracious and takes special pleasure in crashing into our little worlds to offer it. He wields it like a wrecking ball, and it is not always welcome. In fact, Scripture is full of examples of the grace of God prompting anger, confusion, jealousy, self-righteous frustration, and judgment in people. Some find it incredibly offensive, immoral, and totally un-Godlike, but frankly, God couldn't care less. He moves anyway. Our salvation depends upon it. He is more than glad to keep being gracious in the hope that we will someday come around.

To accept grace requires humbleness, which is the primary reason we find it so abrasive. If we refuse to bend low, we cannot receive it. It is particularly hard if we do not see any need for the grace in the first place. But those who do realize their need understand the tremendous gift He has put together for them. And they respond with an arms-wide-open embrace. They take the running leap into His boundless mercy, which is what we call *faith*.

Grace and faith always go together, and always in that order. Faith never precedes God's hand; it receives from Him what He has already set in motion by believing. It takes grace in order to believe. Paul perfectly summed up the relationship between the two for us in Ephesians: "Now God has us where he wants us, with all the time in this world and the next to shower grace and kindness upon us in Christ Jesus. Saving is all his idea, and all his work. All we do is trust him enough to let him do it. It's God's gift from start to finish! We don't play the major role. If we did, we'd probably go around bragging that we'd done the whole thing! No, we neither make nor save ourselves. God does both the making and saving."[1]

The world oozes with the grace of God because He is determined to be kind. It is all around us, threaded through each of our lives, though we are not always able to see it at first. He will stack the deck however necessary to bring us to the point of faith, and if even then we refuse, He remains patiently undeterred. There will always be more grace waiting in the wings.

We can see His dogged persistence in the Old Testament story of Naaman. Naaman was a high-ranking officer in the Syrian army who had wealth, military prowess, family, security, and the esteem of his king. He was an enemy of Israel's. He had also contracted leprosy.[2]

Long before any diagnosis, however, God had already singled out Naaman for mercy. In fact, Scripture tells us He had gone out of His way to bend history and politics in Naaman's favor. Syria conquered Israel under Naaman's leadership because God deliberately arranged it. The Lord also placed a young Israelite girl in his house as a maid. She just so happened to know there was a prophet back home who could heal fatal diseases. She told her mistress, who then told her husband, who, with the permission of the Syrian king, in turn crossed the border to find miracle-working Elisha.

God had placed Naaman on a super highway that led straight to Himself. When the general arrived in Israel, Elisha directed him to simply wash off in the Jordan River. Naaman balked at the command. It was too easy. He expected something far grander and dramatic, something in keeping with the rituals he was used to seeing in his own shamans and medicine men. Why bother coming all this way when there were waters close by in Syria? Elisha did not even offer to accompany him to the riverbank! But all God wanted was for Naaman to step into the Jordan and plunge himself under. We know what that meant: God wanted to include Naaman in Christ, just as He had with His beloved Hebrew people.[3] That was the reason for the repeated onslaught of grace.

Naaman's servants encouraged him to do as the prophet had ordered, and he reluctantly consented. Alone, unceremoniously, and likely feeling more than a bit ridiculous, he waded out into the slow current. He bowed under and instantly met Jesus in the river. He came back up with healthy, restored skin on his hands and limbs. He was more than healed; Scripture attests that his complexion looked like that of a child.

He was so overcome he left the river and headed straight to Elisha's house. Naaman gratefully offered him an enormous gift of gold, silver, and expensive clothes. Under the Spirit's lead, Elisha flatly refused.

"As God lives," Elisha replied, "the God whom I serve, I'll take nothing from you."[4]

Naaman was surprised to hear it but understood what the Man of God was saying. *Nothing.* He nodded. Nothing had been the theme of the day: no fanfare, no logic, no Elisha even present for the miracle. Nothing of

Naaman's own doing had paved the way for him to come face to face with the invisible God who ruled here. It was not even his decision to seek out Elisha. And now this gracious God was asking for nothing in return. He wanted Naaman to continue in nothing. That meant faith, and Naaman was prepared to give it.

"I now know beyond a shadow of a doubt that there is no God anywhere on earth other than the God of Israel,"[5] Naaman confessed. He turned to depart and asked Elisha for shovelfuls of the dirt under his feet, as much as his mules could pack home to Syria. He would continue to worship God from afar. That bare ground would stand witness to nothing, reminding both Naaman and God that he believed.

It is counterintuitive to associate the hand of our Heavenly Father with the dirt, but the ground represents God's grace for us precisely because that is where He told us it would be. "I'm going to provide for you. Go out and look," He said to the wandering Israelites. "Step outside and look beneath your feet."[6]

The next morning, Moses and that host of freed slaves emerged from their tents. Something miraculous had happened. Scripture recalls that the desert sand glittered like diamonds in the faint sunlight:

> *"When the dew evaporated, a flaky substance as fine as frost blanketed the ground. The Israelites were puzzled when they saw it. 'What is it?' they asked each other. They had no idea what it was. And Moses told them, 'It is the food the Lord has given you to eat. These are the Lord's instructions: Each household should gather as much as it needs. Pick up two quarts for each person in your tent.'"*[7]

They grabbed bowls and jars and got to work picking up the bread. They were a homeless nation, a people continually on the move with no land of their own yet to farm. They could not plant crops or wait for an orchard to ripen, and here in the wild desert, nothing grew anyway. They could not count on rainfall or open pasture to support their herds. There were no settlements on their path to buy food from. Bread falling out of the sky was a Godsend of phenomenal proportions, the difference between life and certain death, and all they had to do was look at the ground to find it.

Every morning, God promised, manna would appear at dawn and melt away when the sun reached its zenith. There would always be enough to cover the entire nation's needs for the day. And God was very specific that this was indeed daily bread; if anyone tried to gather more than a day's supply or store it overnight out of fear, the leftovers would spoil and become inedible. The people had no choice but to trust His hand to keep providing. Their journey through the wilderness would be a steady handoff between His grace and their faith.

But just as the people began to depend on the manna, it stopped. Six days in, Moses let them know there would be no bread the following morning. Some went out anyway on the seventh day, only to find the ground bare.

"Every week will be like this," Moses explained to the community. "There will be nothing on the ground on the Sabbath. Don't expect any. In fact, don't even go looking for it. God is commanding that you stay put and completely rest. Do no work at all, in remembrance of His day of rest at creation."

To sustain them through the Sabbath, God promised a second miracle. He would send a double portion on the sixth day, and this would be a different kind of manna that would not spoil overnight. Only on the sixth day would it come, and only then were they to store up extra rations to eat on the Sabbath. They had to learn to trust in total faith that this strange way would be sufficient and that the mysterious bread would return to the ground when the new week dawned.

God kept His word. Both types of manna fell like clockwork for the next four decades, feeding Israel for the duration of its journey into Canaan. Jesus later explained to the hungry and displaced crowd following Him that manna was the Holy Spirit's picture of the Messiah. One type of manna, anyway. For like Jesus, one bread gave life; the other did not. One spoiled, while the other had power to outlast rot and decay—power it shared with anyone who ate it. He told them, "Do not work for food that spoils, but for food that endures to eternal life, which the Son of Man will give you. For on him God the Father has placed his seal of approval."[8]

To prove His point, Jesus took a single portion of food and multiplied it exponentially for the crowd. He had them sit on the ground, signaling He was ready to unveil His grace, and asked His disciples to distribute the food. Thousands ate all they wanted, and Jesus sent the disciples once more through the crowd to collect any bits of bread that were leftover. They returned with twelve heaping baskets, enough for all twelve tribes of Israel to eat another day. It was more than reminiscent of Israel's time in the wilderness. It was a carbon copy of the miraculous, unspoiling, day-before-the-Sabbath manna. God had deliberately sent them an extra portion, and He meant for them to pay attention to that.[9]

John notes, however, that the wonder's meaning was utterly lost on the crowd. Just as the ancients had done so many centuries before, many got up the next morning with rumbling stomachs and instinctively looked for Jesus. They came to the same ground where He had fed them in anticipation of more bread. Same as their ancestors, they found only bare dirt.

Jesus was not there. Overnight, He had crossed the lake for Capernaum. He had walked on water while the disciples battled a tempest and, in doing so, revealed His imminent death-killing death.[10] John wants us to understand that this day was the real Sabbath. This was the day Bread no longer covered the ground, the day that no one could work to gather it. It was the day the Lord Himself rested in a tomb. It was the day grace appeared to be gone, but was in fact superabundantly provided. It was a day that called for real faith.

But the people simply could not understand it. Discontented, they quickly crossed the lake after Jesus. They found Him on the far shore and demanded He provide another free meal. "Give us that bread every day!"[11] they whined, and when He refused, they grew even crankier. Some argued back, and some quit following altogether.

Jesus didn't flinch. He needed them to see that the Bread He provided was enough, for the miraculous meal had foreshadowed the cross. There was no need for everyday bread ever again. Their great need was now to believe it, to believe Him, for only by faith could they access the life the Bread was offering. He laid everything out for them as clearly as He could:

> *"I'm telling you the most solemn and sober truth now: Whoever believes in me has real life, eternal life. I am the Bread of Life. Your ancestors ate the manna bread in the desert and died. But now here is Bread that truly comes down out of heaven. Anyone eating this Bread will not die, ever. I am the Bread—living Bread!—who came down out of heaven. Anyone who eats this Bread will live—and forever! The Bread that I present to the*

world so that it can eat and live is myself, this flesh-and-blood self... Only insofar as you eat and drink flesh and blood, the flesh and blood of the Son of Man, do you have life within you. The one who brings a hearty appetite to this eating and drinking has eternal life and will be fit and ready for the Final Day. My flesh is real food and my blood is real drink. By eating my flesh and drinking my blood you enter into me and I into you. In the same way that the fully alive Father sent me here and I live because of him, so the one who makes a meal of me lives because of me. This is the Bread from heaven. Your ancestors ate bread and later died. Whoever eats this Bread will live always."[12]

Many disciples turned and walked away from Jesus after the Feeding of the Five Thousand. The grace of God can seem so repugnant when it conflicts with what we want out of God. We long for daily bread, when He has provided eternal sustenance. We look at the bare ground and charge Him with wrongdoing. He says that very dirt is proof of His grace.

Jesus once was in Jerusalem for a festival and passed through a section of the city called Bethesda. It must have been a beautiful sight architecturally. Scripture records a large pool was nestled there under five arched alcoves, flanked by open spaces that could accommodate hundreds of people. Hundreds of people were indeed gathered when Jesus walked by, for the pool was famous for its healing powers. The sick, lame, and broken crowded around it, hoping to see the waters stir and bubble up. That was the indicator an angel had come down from heaven, so the story goes, sent to make the first person who stepped into the pool completely well again.[13]

Jesus met a man as He lingered there who had waited by the waters for thirty-eight years. He told Jesus he had seen it happen. The waters had moved and the bubbles had risen to the surface, but due to his disabilities, he had never been able to get in quick enough. Someone else always got in first and snagged the miracle.

He, like all the others, was lying on the ground watching for grace to make itself known. He was stretched out on a thin sleeping mat. How Jesus chose him from among the rest, Scripture does not say. But the Lord took notice, crouched down, and asked with deep compassion, "Do you want to get well?"[14]

The man's eyes panned over to the pool, and with a sigh, he told Jesus he had no one to help him into the water. Jesus interpreted that response as a yes. "Stand up!" He said suddenly. "Get up and take the mat with you!" Without missing a beat, the man did as he was told. He rose to his feet, stuffed his bedroll under his arm, and started walking around.

It was identical to the Feeding of the Five Thousand: a sort of anti-miracle that resulted in permanent provision. Curiously, no one seems to have noticed. Those waiting by the waters continued to watch them; no one even turned their head when the paralyzed man stood up. They were all looking for bubbles, for the moment when that little sea transformed into living water. The problem was, it was only temporary. It was bread that spoiled. Every time the angel stirred it, the pool eventually stilled and became a sea once more. It could not really give life, though it was the best hope the sick and lame had yet found. They all stared at the featureless pool, while the man danced about in joy behind their backs.

He, on the other hand, had tasted resurrection. His body had been as good as dead, bound with paralysis, and now he was alive, up and utterly free. He held in his hands the mat he had lain on for so many years. There was an empty spot on the portico where the mat had been. That bare patch of ground shined like a beacon for the other invalids still stretched out under the alcoves. It called out for everyone to notice.

But it was not the ground that caught people's attention, nor the happiness the man exuded as he waltzed through the city streets. It was the rolled-up mat under his arm. The Pharisees noticed it immediately and pulled him aside for questioning. For this day, like the one following the Feeding of the Five Thousand, was a Sabbath, and carrying a mat around was considered an illegal activity. It was work.

The man had no explanation to offer, other than Jesus had told him explicitly to take it with him and go. "The man who healed me told me, 'Pick up your mat and walk.'"[15] He shrugged his shoulders and waltzed on.

Jesus knew it would make them furious. He meant it to provoke them and welcomed their irritated interrogation when they came to Him next. The secret, of course, was that the man had not broken the Sabbath at all. He had done nothing other than believe Jesus's words, a literal nothing. Carrying a mat was not work; it was faith, a faith that pointed squarely back to Jesus. The one laboring here was God.

"This is the only 'work' God wants from you: Believe in the one he has sent," He pressed on the crowd.[16] Faith.

The healed man was a picture of Christ Himself, one that Jesus deeply wanted the Pharisees to grapple with. He had rested on the ground like a corpse for far too long. He had also deliberately rested from work by trusting God to raise him. Now, he was dancing like a ballerina and waving his bedroll as a banner, and the ground was suspiciously bare. What else was the Sabbath for? It was a holy day commemorating the Lord's rest, the day Jesus lay still in absolute faith God would not abandon His Son in the grave.

"Pick up your mat and walk." To our ears, Jesus's direction should sound like, "If any of you wants to be my follower, you must give up your own way, take up your cross daily, and follow me."[17] That was what this man had in his hands, a cross. It looked like a dirty and long-used sleeping mat, but it was really a cross lifted in public declaration: "This is the man who made me well! Here is how it happened!"

We are holding a cross, and some of us plod along as if we were on our way out to be crucified. Child, crucifixion has already happened, and you were there with Him through faith. Simply pick up the cross and embrace it. His cross is your cross too. You are not being led out to death; you are on your way back from the grave. That ground where He lay is bare, and yours will be too. All He is asking is that we believe.

The wondrous thing about that dirt is that it is not really bare at all. It looks abandoned and unloved, but the truth is that there is no more grace-soaked place on the face of the earth. Bare ground is the stage for resurrection, both a testimony that it will happen and a monument that it already has. We ought to look up, fully expectant for God's power to break loose when we come across it. He will transform the humble dirt beyond all recognition until what we see matches all we have believed:

> *"The desert and the parched land will be glad; the wilderness will rejoice and blossom. Like the crocus, it will burst into bloom; it will rejoice greatly and shout for joy. The glory of Lebanon will be given to it, the splendor of Carmel and Sharon; they will see the glory of the Lord, the splendor of our God... Water will gush forth*

> *in the wilderness and streams in the desert. The burning sand will become a pool, the thirsty ground bubbling springs. In the haunts where jackals once lay, grass and reeds and papyrus will grow. And a highway will be there; it will be called the Way of Holiness; it will be for those who walk on that Way...those the Lord has rescued will return."*[18]

How will they return? Resurrection. That has always been God's plan. Grace upon grace until faith becomes sight. Across Scripture, we see hints that the badlands are secretly stocked with His richest blessings. When Abraham parted with Lot because their pastures could no longer support two herds, Lot chose the green fields to the east.[19] This left Abraham with the barren ground to the west. God made a surprise appearance to reassure his friend he had gotten the far better end of the deal. He told Abraham, "Open your eyes, look around. Look north, south, east, and west. Everything you see, the whole land spread out before you, I will give to you and your children forever. I'll make your descendants like dust—counting your descendants will be as impossible as counting the dust of the Earth. So—on your feet, get moving! Walk through the country, its length and breadth; I'm giving it all to you."[20]

When Isaac was harassed by the Philistines and forced to find new places to camp, the wild ground yielded well after well of life-giving water. He faced constant hostility as a stranger living in a strange land, but God had already laid out a network of springs hidden for him to find in each time of need.[21]

When Jesus encountered a man blind from birth, He spit on the ground to make mud. With the skilled hands of a Potter, He added that clay to His prized creation. He spread it over the man's sightless eyes, carefully reframing and shaping his face, sculpting him anew. The man washed the mud off and for the first time beheld every stroke of color and shade the visible world had to offer. "This happened so that the works of God might be displayed in him,"[22] Jesus explained. The bare ground was laid there for it.[23]

And when Joram started a senseless war with Moab out in the baking wilderness, God proved kind. He gave extravagant grace to a king who should have known Him but refused to bow. God provided water to his thirsty troops and horses from an unseen source. Without so much as a raindrop, the dry valley became a pool and revealed the whole of God's plan for salvation.[24]

The sun rose over that water, turning it red like blood. The ground was streaked with it, crying out not for divine vengeance but for forgiveness. "Why should the Lord rescue Israel's faithless and idolatrous king? What do the king and the Lord have in common?" Elisha asked. Joram saw Christ in the dirt and Israel won the battle against Moab that day, but even then, he would not believe. God poured out His grace anyway. That is His way.

The ground pointed ahead to the quiet early morning Jesus spent in Gethsemane, where blood dripped from His forehead and mixed with the lowly dirt. The stress was breaking Him. The cross loomed at dawn, and He knelt in fervent prayer.[25]

Three times He asked the Father if this terrible suffering could pass from Him, with Peter, James, and John watching Him pray. He received His answer from heaven. Almost instantly, His betrayer arrived, and Jesus stood up willingly to meet him.

Understand that there were an infinite number of other ways God could have saved us, for as Jesus declared in His prayer, everything is possible for God. It is *nothing* that is impossible. He could have spared His Son the pain of crucifixion, but He did not. Jesus asked His friends to watch Him pray for this very reason. The cry that came from Jesus's lips was not one of fear or last-minute reluctance, and neither was our God painted into a corner and unable to rescue His Son without losing us. Where would God's immense love be if that were the case? The prayer was for us, for reassurance. Jesus also added, "I want what You want, Abba. Do what You will." And in that, He revealed this grace was indeed the Father's decision. Out of His endless wisdom and eternal goodness, Jesus's blood was the sole way the Father had chosen to forgive us. Jesus wanted all His disciples to know it. Beyond the shadow of any doubt, His blood is the only salvation God will ever make available to humanity. We must trust it. By grace, that blood appeared before any hand rose up to attack Him. It had always been there. In fact, all the universe had been built on that blood, set upon Him like a building on its cornerstone. Jesus is "the Lamb who was slain from the creation of the world."[26] The ground we stand upon is proof.

Peter would later reflect:

> *"This was no afterthought. Even though it has only lately—at the end of the ages—become public knowledge, God always knew he*

was going to do this for you. It's because of this sacrificed Messiah, whom God then raised from the dead and glorified, that you trust God, that you know you have a future in God."[27]

The ground is never bare. Look with faith, and you too will see nothing and be made strong. Believe when you hear the stunned reports, "He isn't here! He is risen from the dead, just as He said would happen."[28] Believe, for that ground is where resurrection has blossomed.

---

1 Ephesians 2:7–9 MSG
2 This story occurs in 2 Kings 5.
3 See Chapter 2 for more on this.
4 2 Kings 5:16 MSG
5 2 Kings 5:15 MSG
6 This story occurs in Exodus 16.
7 Exodus 16:14–16 NLT
8 John 6:27 NIV
9 This story occurs in Matthew 14, Mark 6, Luke 9, and John 6.
10 See Chapter 1 for more on this.
11 John 6:34 NLT
12 John 6:47–51, 53–58 MSG
13 This story occurs in John 5.
14 John 5:6 NIV
15 John 5:11 NLT
16 John 6:29 NLT
17 Luke 9:23 NLT
18 Isaiah 35:1–2, 6–8, 10 NIV
19 This story occurs in Genesis 13.
20 Genesis 13:14–17 MSG
21 This story occurs in Genesis 26.
22 John 9:3 NIV
23 This story occurs in John 9.
24 This story occurs in 2 Kings 3.
25 This story occurs in Luke 22.
26 Revelation 13:8 NIV
27 1 Peter 1:18–21 NLT
28 Matthew 28:6 NLT

CHAPTER SIX

A Sower Went Out to Sow

"For you have been born again, not of perishable seed,
but of imperishable, through the living and enduring word of God. For,
'All people are like grass, and all their glory is like the flowers of the field;
the grass withers and the flowers fall, but the word of the
Lord endures forever.' And this is the word that was preached to you."

– 1 Peter 1:23–25 NIV

There was a point on that third glorious day when the Creator looked over the length and width of the land. In the morning sunlight, I can picture Him tipping back the brim of His hat and crouching down to pick up clumps of fresh turned dirt. For the first time, the universe gave off a damp, earthy scent. Imagine how wonderful it smelled as He crumbled the soil through His fingers. All around, it smelled of spring under a rain-washed sky. The ground was ready now. Planting could begin.

He scanned the field's borders. He estimated the seed He would need, silently figuring yield versus loss. Some, He knew, would root but not flower. Some, the birds would gobble up. Still there was some that would seize His grace with fervor and overcome all odds to reach maturity. The harvest would be beyond counting, multiplying again and again a hundred times over. He reached His hand gently into the pouch slung over His shoulder and got to work scattering seeds.

Day three signaled a ringing triumph. The Son was raised to life on day three, and with it came the guarantee that we would be raised in resurrection with Him. Our future is as sure and solid as His, though what it will look like is still anyone's wildest guess:

> *"But someone may ask, 'How will the dead be raised? What kind of bodies will they have?' What a foolish question! When you put a seed into the ground, it doesn't grow into a plant unless it dies first. And what you put in the ground is not the plant that will grow, but only a bare seed of wheat or whatever you are planting. Then God gives it the new body he wants it to have. A different plant grows from each kind of seed... It is the same way with the resurrection of the dead. Our earthly bodies are planted in the ground when we die, but they will be raised to live forever. Our bodies are buried in brokenness, but they will be raised in glory. They are buried in weakness, but they will be raised in strength."*[1]

In the most beautiful way possible, we have absolutely no idea what God has in store for us. All we have for now is the seed, the word God planted within us, and we should not misjudge by its humble appearance. James tells us the word is explosively powerful and can save our souls. An entire forest is tucked away inside it.

But seeds have a monumental task set before them. There is a long gap between a tiny seed and a towering redwood, and the journey is full of opposition. For a seed to germinate, it must be buried. Water triggers the magic process hidden under the husk. The root secretly emerges, and a tender shoot springs upward. A pair of bright green leaves flank the little stem as it steadily climbs taller. The young plant is wholly dependent on its conditions. Too much light, and it will wither. Too much water, and it will rot. Too little of either, and it will not grow.

It is a metaphor running throughout Scripture for our fragile lives and a favorite teaching illustration of Jesus. And the point is straightforward. Our growth is directly tied to God's ongoing provision. We need Him continually and should learn to look for His hand in trusting expectation.

This is an organic process, because faith is a life built on grace. God compared faith to a journey taken a step at a time, Him walking with us at a leisurely pace. There must be a continued reliance on His grace for faith to function: He provides; we receive. He leads; we trust. He teaches; we grow. He prunes, and we bear fruit. The cycle repeats because He is always faithful. Grace, and then faith.

It means that faith must follow the word's arrival in the heart. Like a thorough watering, the seed will sprout only if we respond to it in willing faith. Ears that don't hear with faith are like ground baked hard as a brick. The scattered seed piles up on the surface, the birds make off with it, and no change results from the grace. A trusting heart, on the other hand, unleashes the word and roots begin to form.

So, when He plants, it's up to us to listen. Our only part is to do what Jesus is saying: "Whoever has ears to hear, let them hear."[2] We must believe.

In the Parable of the Sower, Jesus demonstrates this dynamic relationship of grace and faith with four types of soil. The first was like concrete, unplowed and unreceptive. He had in mind the narrow footpaths that stripe a wheat field. This is where the Farmer walks between the rows as He does His work. The dirt is tightly compacted and not used for planting. When some seed fell from the Farmer's hand onto this soil, Jesus said nothing grew. The ground was too hard. The seed never entered it, representing ears that do not hear. It is a warning that unbelief will germinate nothing.[3]

The second and third soils did better. Both listened, yet their seeds still struggled mightily after planting. The second soil was shallow and rocky, which meant the emergent seedling never developed strong roots. It sprouted and was quickly scorched under a hostile sun. Thorns and weeds crowded the third bed of soil, choking the little plant when it came up. It also died, Jesus said, suffocated by the relentless waves of anxiety life throws at us.

We might look at this sorry garden and conclude it was all a waste. None of the three soils were able to sustain a plant to maturity, and none produced any fruit. Why would the Farmer even bother to scatter seeds? Why should we bother to listen when He does? Can we expect anything better? But writing off His word would be a terrible mistake on our part. That is not what God sees; in fact, He looks at the withered plants and stubbornly claims just the opposite. He looks at the garden and continues to declare, "The word of God will never fail."[4] He has staked His name and eternal reputation on its power.

God is neither a liar nor delusional, and to understand what He means we must turn to what He revealed to Isaiah. The key lies in understanding *who* the parable is actually about, and the answer is that it is not about us, at least not entirely. The struggling little plants Jesus describes are a picture of Himself. Hundreds of years before His birth, God let Isaiah see that the Messiah's life would be one of tremendous pain, opposition—and apparent failure:

> *"My servant grew up in the Lord's presence like a tender green shoot, like a root in dry ground. There was nothing beautiful or majestic about his appearance, nothing to attract us to him. He was despised and rejected—a man of sorrows, acquainted with deepest grief. We turned our backs on him and looked the other way. He was despised, and we did not care… He was oppressed and treated harshly, yet he never said a word. He was led like a lamb to the slaughter. And as a sheep is silent before the shearers, he did not open his mouth. Unjustly condemned, he was led away. No one cared that he died without descendants, that his life was cut short in midstream."*[5]

A tender shoot; a root in dry ground. In other words, doomed from the start. We must not forget that the persecution Jesus encountered was so severe He died under it. He died a very young man, a good, godly man who had no children or earthly kingdom to carry on His name. He died in disgrace never seeing fruit from His obedience or the fulfillment of God's many promises. He was the seedling that sprouted among the rocks only to wilt under the fierce midday sun. He grew exactly where God had planted Him in that second bed of soil.

And Isaiah saw it was not persecution alone that would take Jesus's life; he saw that the anxieties, worries, and lusts plaguing the third bed of soil were also piled on Him. He saw sin heaped on Jesus and choke Him at the cross, though Jesus was innocent of committing any wrong. He saw every weakness of ours and every shame wrap themselves like tendrils around Jesus, as if it were us in His place hanging there. He watched Jesus let it happen without a word of protest:

> *"Yet it was our weaknesses he carried; it was our sorrows that weighed him down. And we thought his troubles were a punishment*

> *from God, a punishment for his own sins! But he was pierced for our rebellion, crushed for our sins. He was beaten so we could be whole. He was whipped so we could be healed."*[6]

It is Jesus in the parable. He did not reach maturity here on earth. By God's perfect plan He did not and could not, because God intended all along for Him to die as the sacrifice offered in our place. What looked like disaster to the world was total triumph in God's eyes, the sign of everything going exactly to plan

And that plan was never going to end in death for Jesus, though it most certainly would go through it. There was resurrection imminently ahead. There had to be! How else could the Father make good on all He owed the Son, all the fruit Jesus deserved but had been unjustly denied? How else could God boast, "[My word] will not return to me empty, but will accomplish what I desire and achieve the purpose for which I sent it"? Resurrection was the only way.[7]

God swore to raise Jesus, and by resurrection to give Him the immense joy of real life, with billions upon billions of descendants to share in it—you and I, and all our brothers and sisters across the Church:

> *"Still, it's what God had in mind all along, to crush him with pain. The plan was that he give himself as an offering for sin so that he'd see life come from it—life, life, and more life. And God's plan will deeply prosper through him. Out of that terrible travail of soul, he'll see that it's worth it and be glad he did it. Through what he experienced, my righteous one, my servant, will make many 'righteous ones,' as he himself carries the burden of their sins. Therefore I'll reward him extravagantly—the best of everything, the highest honors—Because he looked death in the face and didn't flinch, because he embraced the company of the lowest. He took on his own shoulders the sin of the many, he took up the cause of all the black sheep."*[6]

What a harvest was ready and waiting for Him beyond the grave, a harvest the Father was more than ready to pour out! For there is also a fourth soil in the Parable of the Sower, a good soil that is clean, fertile, and thistle-free. And this ground, Jesus promised, *will* produce a fantastic harvest, as certainly as the others did not. Rich topsoil like this is the painstaking handiwork of an expert Farmer. It is not naturally occurring, as any gardener can attest. This is soil that has been lovingly cared for and deliberately prepared. Every dandelion plucked, every rock excavated, every invasive briar yanked out by the roots. Everything plaguing us has been laid on Him at the cross. The grace this soil represents is so divinely extravagant the seed is guaranteed to flourish. It is a picture of the Risen Christ and our lives in Him. We are that fourth soil because of all He endured. The word did not fail.

You and I might look at ourselves and beg to differ. Depression and disappointment might be running rampant. We might consider our lives anything but free or productive. Maybe there are trails of disaster behind us or walls of insurmountable opposition on every side. We've prayed, yet they haven't budged. We've watched patiently, but no good has come of what the Lord promised He would do through us. The green hope that sprang up has been neglected and crushed. Perhaps it is long since dead, and we are baffled as we mourn it. All we can conclude is that He failed.

This is where faith must be put to work. Not to pretend our troubles are small or that we can overcome on our own—what garden can weed itself? That is not faith, and it is the exact opposite of what God is asking of us. Faith is deliberate trust in God's grace, and God has declared that because of Jesus a boundless harvest is ours. He says the fourth ground is ready and the grace is sufficient. Do we believe Him? Do we believe He can do it, though all we see are our messy and underwhelming lives?

The seed, remember, is the word. What the Father has planted in us is the gospel, the message of Jesus Christ crucified. It is a *resurrection seed*, and, Child, when it sprouts, it will live again even though it dies. Resurrection is what is planted deep within you, and it will certainly reach abundance. The tiniest flicker of faith is enough to unleash it.

"Son of man, can these bones live?" Ezekiel looked around. It was the Holy Spirit asking, but all Ezekiel could see were thousands upon thousands of dead bones littering the valley floor. They were so old and dead the sun had bleached them bare, so uprooted and severed from grace they were not even buried. The ground was carpeted with them, the same ground they had once been formed from, where God had once sculpted the rich soil into human beings filled with His own life. Now they lay lifeless among the patches of grassy stubble, still and silent as an early snowfall.[9]

Ezekiel knew the obvious answer as he walked through the valley. Dead bones do not live. They *have lived*, but hope failed and life fled. No one can change that, whether on earth or in heaven.

But can they live again? So many bones were dotting the landscape. "Master God, only you know that,"[10] the prophet admitted.

God was pressing for something firmer. He needed Ezekiel to decide. He needed Ezekiel, and by extension, every one of us, to come face to face with the stark reality of death and decide where the limits of God's power fell.

Ezekiel looked at them again, wondering. The wind was softly picking up. "Speak to the bones, Ezekiel," the Spirit said. "Speak the word over them. Tell them who I am—that I am the LORD, the Alive." The Holy Spirit continued, "Say, 'I'm bringing the breath of life to you and you'll come to life. I'll attach sinews to you, put meat on your bones, cover you with skin, and breathe life into you. You'll come alive and you'll realize that I am God!'"[11]

Ezekiel gave them His message. As he did, the wind started to roar. The bones rustled in the dry grass. He watched as an unseen hand snapped them back together like magnets, forming perfect skeletons. He watched skin and silken muscle clothe them. He heard the Spirit rush into the renewed bodies as at creation. Before him suddenly was a living multitude taking deep, steady breaths and replanted on solid ground.

Ezekiel had seen resurrection. His God was able to do it; he now knew that in his own bones. There was no question remaining if He could raise dried out and empty lives, or whether He wanted to, or whether He would. His strength and compassion were absolute. God knew Ezekiel needed to see resurrection in order to believe it. Grace always precedes faith.

But the prophet had been shown so much more than God's raw power. He had just seen God's plan, which was God Himself. This vision was a portrait. Ezekiel was looking directly at God's face.

"You'll come alive and you'll realize that I am God," the Lord declared. It was a revelation that seeing resurrection is seeing the invisible God, for Resurrection is not an event. He is a Person.

"*I* am the Resurrection," Jesus told a grieving and bewildered Martha. They were standing together near her brother Lazarus's tomb. He had been buried earlier in the week, and the ache was painfully fresh for everyone.[12]

Jesus had just arrived from out of town. He had not been there when Lazarus died, nor had he been there when Lazarus fell sick, nor when Martha and her sister Mary did what they could to nurse him back to health. He had missed it all, though they had sent Him urgent word to come quickly and heal Lazarus. Their brother had died waiting for Him to come, and the two women had gone numb enduring His glaring absence.

John was with Jesus when He first learned of Lazarus's illness and remembered His striking response to the news. Jesus said, "This sickness will not end in death. No, it is for God's glory so that God's Son may be glorified through it."[13] And then, even more perplexing, John tells us Jesus stayed where He was for two more days. He hunkered down and deliberately did not stir. The Holy Spirit grabbed John and said to pay close attention.

For two more days, bringing the total to three, He remained totally sedentary, a picture of the unthinkable weekend of crucifixion and death just ahead for Himself. Lazarus's need was dire, more so than anyone other than Jesus yet realized, and it only deepened His resolve to push on to the cross. Lazarus needed Him to stay. His life depended on it, and Jesus deeply loved him. "This is for the glory of God, for the Son's glory," Jesus stubbornly declared, claiming divine territory like an explorer planting a flag. Glory is resurrection talk, and a final warning shot for death to prepare for battle. Translation: "Only resurrection will cure this sickness—*My* resurrection. I will not let up or be moved."

And so, He stayed. No one understood, least of all Mary and Martha, who were clinging to His love and anxiously watching for His shadow on the doorstep. At last, on the third day, He announced to the disciples it was time to get up and get going. "Our friend Lazarus has fallen asleep; but I am going there to wake him up."[14] Lazarus had died during those three silent days, and the disciples could not wrap their minds around why Jesus would bother going to him now. But Jesus was insistent. It was Day Three, and God was ready to unveil His Resurrection.

By the time they completed the journey to Lazarus's village, he had been in the tomb a full four days. It was an ugly scene they came upon. Around the gravesite, disheveled mourners stood in deep distress: family, friends, neighbors, and the obligatory religious busybodies. Tears were flowing and heartfelt consolations were being rejected in the face of angry, unanswerable questions.

Jesus's arrival did not go unnoticed. All the crowd could ask was what took Him so long. "He opened the eyes of a blind man!" they murmured to one other. "Why didn't He come in time?" The sisters had words for Him too. "If you had only been here, our brother would not have died!"

Mary fell at His feet, sobbing in pain and unable to say anything further. Wails echoed all around her, and Jesus broke down too. He began to cry hard, for He genuinely did love this family. Lest we ever think God is indifferent about our losses, or that we ought to be as people of faith, we need to visit this scene again and again. He wept, and not just in sympathy. He had lost Lazarus too. There is no one who despises death like He does. It is Godlike to weep in a cemetery.

But as the tears fell, another emotion began to rise in Jesus. Fury churned deep in His spirit. He looked at the tomb, which was a small hillside cave covered with a slab of rock, and then back at the people huddled around it in their grief. That angry hurricane grew stronger. Martha noticed the change in His demeanor and became nervous.

He marched up to the cave and demanded someone pull back the stone for Him. Horrorstruck, Martha jumped up too. She gently tried to reel Him back to reality. Perhaps He had lost track of the timeline. Perhaps He had simply lost His mind. "Jesus, he's been dead half a week! The stench will be unbearable," she protested.

He looked at her with a look she would never forget. "Didn't I tell you that you would see the glory of God here? Open it." He was not taking no for an answer.

Martha was right to be alarmed. It was like standing on an active volcano as the pressure built in Jesus's heart. Something catastrophic was brewing before their eyes. She had never seen this side of Jesus. No one had, for God was revealing something gloriously new. This was a vision of Day Three Jesus, the Resurrection who had conquered death and now held all power to free its captives.

Why was He angry? What could the Risen Christ have to be angry about? Never in Scripture is God's anger a good thing. Sin is what ignites God's white-hot anger, and the longer sin persists, the more dangerous it grows. But this is Day Three Jesus. This Jesus walked up to the cave with nail-pierced feet. His hands and forehead had scars from the cross and the tangled crown of thorns. This Jesus, the Holy Spirit wants us to see, had already taken the punishment and satisfied the demands of divine justice. Sin had been dealt with.

This was the result: the Resurrection standing in a graveyard, simultaneously weeping and fuming over what He saw. The anger coursing through Jesus was not wrath over sin, for that wrath had been poured out on day one at the cross. This was anger over unbelief. One by one, Jesus turned to the mourners to ask if they believed. The disciples certainly did not. They did not understand the sign God was revealing in the slightest and saw only disaster surrounding Him. When Jesus told them it was time to go raise Lazarus, Thomas shrugged his shoulders and said to the others, "Come along. We might as well die with him."[15] They did not understand that resurrection was Jesus's plan for Lazarus, and that He Himself was that Resurrection.

The crowd gathered at the tomb was full of skeptical priests and Pharisees who refused to put faith of any kind in Jesus. Time and time again, they had seen His works and heard His teachings, but they would not believe.

Mary had been deeply devoted to Jesus. She had once sat at His feet and ignored all other responsibilities in the name of drawing closer to Him. But Lazarus's death had broken her. She had given up on Him in bitter frustration and would not even greet Him when He arrived in Bethany. Martha did best of all. She met Him right away, despite her sorrow. When Jesus pressed her, she said she still believed He was the Messiah, but stopped short of connecting that Lordship to Resurrection. It was beyond her too to believe at that level.

He was standing right before them, but no one saw who He truly was. No one understood, and therefore no one believed. Some could not, because of pain or ignorance; some would not, because they preferred to stay blind. Jesus looked around, angry. And that anger led Him to do something extraordinary.

"Roll back the stone!" He told them.

In the Parable of the Sower, there was a soil so tough the seed could not take root. The seed could not enter the ground and simply piled up on the footpaths as bird food. The soil needed to be worked before being planted; why would a Farmer skip that crucial first step? Trust that He does not.

Unbelief locks the seed out of the heart, and our God is determined there will be a harvest. Wherever the ground is hard, you can rest assured that is where He will be diligently at work plowing. On the way to Lazarus's village, Jesus told His disciples, "Are there not twelve hours of daylight? Anyone who walks in daylight doesn't stumble because there's plenty of light from the sun. Walking at night, he might very well stumble because he can't see where he's going."[16] He knew everyone who cared for Lazarus, the disciples included, needed a better faith to make it through the agony of death, both Lazarus's and in time, their own.

That faith was a new faith, and it could only arise from a new grace. They needed to believe in resurrection, but like Ezekiel, first they needed to see it. Everyone does. God first needed to cut furrows into the hard ground so the seed could take root. He needed to reveal His Son.

Standing before that open grave, Jesus raised His eyes in prayer. He had one request of His Father: that those watching would believe God sent Him. "Let them believe!" He asked. And then He shouted for Lazarus to come out. Right on cue, the dead man did. They all watched as the seedling burst up from the ground. He was wrapped in linen strips, and his face was obscured by a cloth, but Lazarus was fully alive again. He hobbled out of the cave to stunned faces and grateful cheers.

The miracle was for Mary, for Martha, for Thomas and John; for the members of Lazarus's extended family who suddenly reaped joy from their tears; for all the cynics and those who opposed Jesus relentlessly; for those who waffled and could not make up their minds about Him; for anyone who has heard Jesus's name but does not yet grasp who He is. Scripture tells us Lazarus became a walking exhibit for the Resurrection. People put their faith in Jesus right and left, so much so that His enemies plotted to put Lazarus in the grave a second time to quiet the chatter.

It was a revelation Mary, above all, took to heart. She and Martha threw a banquet to celebrate Lazarus's new lease on life and to thank Jesus publicly. As the guests were eating and talking away, Mary quietly knelt before Him. In her hands was an expensive heirloom, a jar of fine perfume that had been passed down for generations in her family. Under the Holy Spirit's lead, she broke the jar and poured out every drop on His feet. Conversation halted as the fragrance overpowered the room. Soon the whole house smelled sweet with it. She had anointed Christ, not for a throne, but for burial. She knew He was the Resurrection and now understood things do not stay dead around Him. There would be no stench of death on Jesus heading into the grave or returning from it, nor would there be for anyone else united with Him ever again.[17]

Ultimately, of course, the miracle was for Lazarus. It is the dead who need resurrection, those who are dead physically or dead in some other metaphorical and equally hopeless way. Wounded spirits, listen and take heart, for our God can indeed open eyes and keep a man from dying. He can also raise the dead. Shattered dreams, barren promises, dry bones: all of these are candidates for resurrection. It is who He is.

Lest we look at our gravestones and doubt His name, we have the example of Elijah. After the showdown on Mount Carmel, his body and spirit gave out. The queen of Israel reaffirmed the death threat against him, and the endless persecution so rattled mighty Elijah that he quit. He resigned his post as prophet, ran to the desert, collapsed under a shade tree, and asked God to let him die on the spot.[18]

The Lord had no such desire for His lonely and weary child. He sent an angel down with food and water and directed Elijah to walk to Mount Horeb. There, new grace would be poured out. Elijah crawled into a cave on the summit and slept, looking every bit a dead man in his tomb. In the morning God's voice roused him, calling Elijah to stand up. He was going to reveal Himself, the Resurrection, for that was Elijah's true need.

God said to watch. Elijah braced as a gale swept over the mountain and rocks began to break loose overhead. No sooner had it died down than the ground beneath him rumbled and groaned. The mountain shook with a sudden earthquake. He grabbed hold of whatever he could to stay upright. Next a fire blazed out, forcing Elijah to jump farther back into the cave for cover.

A gentle whisper then came to Elijah, somewhere deep inside the recesses of the cavern, and as soon as he heard it, Elijah knew His God was present. He covered his face with his cloak, in both worshipful deference and hugely prophetic imagery, and came out of the cave's mouth. He looked like a corpse raised up, still partially wrapped in burial cloths.

Scripture takes peculiar pains to tell us God was not in the fire, the earthquake, or the shattering windstorm. He was in the whisper, there with Elijah in the grave. He was the invitation beckoning the prophet to come back out and reenter life.

The whisper said, "What are you doing here, Elijah?"[19] It was a question ripe with meaning, and the answer was that Elijah was standing on holy ground with His God. Grace had led him to the very place Jesus stood, with Him in unexpected resurrection. "Go back the same way you came,"[20] the Lord continued. There was a whole second lifetime of ministry awaiting him, full of hope, faith, and community. "You came here by death, but death has now become your entrance into life. What looked like a dead end has become a door. Get going!" Elijah didn't wait another moment.

Can you hear it as well, the gentle whisper on the mountain? It drowns out the crash of rockslides and earthquakes, for after they have done their worst and run out of breath, God's love for us is still here and remains unchanged. By grace it calls your name and mine. It meets us in our deepest need and will rip apart any barrier that blocks out faith. It can move a gravestone. It is the Son's voice, rich in mercy, saying, "Child, drenched in holy love, come out of there! Rise up!"

---

1 1 Corinthians 15:35–38, 42–43 NLT
2 Mark 4:9 NIV
3 This story occurs in Mark 4, Luke 8, and Matthew 13.
4 Luke 1:37 NLT
5 Isaiah 53:2–3, 7–8 NLT
6 Isaiah 53:4–5 NLT
7 Isaiah 55:11 NIV
8 Isaiah 53:10–12 MSG
9 This story occurs in Ezekiel 37.
10 Ezekiel 37:3 MSG
11 Ezekiel 37:5–6 MSG
12 This story occurs in John 11.
13 John 11:4 NIV
14 John 11:11 NIV
15 John 11:16 MSG
16 John 11:9–10 MSG
17 This story occurs in Matthew 26, Mark 14, and John 12.
18 This story occurs in 1 Kings 19.
19 1 Kings 19:13 NIV
20 1 Kings 19:15 NLT

Picture Three: *Robe*

CHAPTER SEVEN

Your Father Knows You Need Them

"Christ's love makes the church whole. His words evoke her beauty. Everything he does and says is designed to bring the best out of her, dressing her in dazzling white silk, radiant with holiness."

– Ephesians 5:25–27 MSG

Oh, the love of God! That never failing, always patient, ever hopeful, eternally unprovoked, and relentlessly extended essence constituting our ineffable God. Father, Son, and Spirit are who He is, but love answers the fundamental *what*. God is love, John tells us, after a lifetime considering the matter.

He testifies:

> *"From the very first day, we were there, taking it all in—we heard it with our own ears, saw it with our own eyes, verified it with our own hands. The Word of Life appeared right before our eyes; we saw it happen! And now we're telling you in most sober prose that what we witnessed was, incredibly, this: The infinite Life of God himself took shape before us."* [1]

The form God assumed was love, undiluted love in its full strength and purity. For love takes its definition from God, specifically Christ stretching out His hands on the cross. "This is how we know what love is: Jesus Christ laid down his life for us."[2] That is love's only meaning.

And though love permeates our world and dominates our thoughts and desires, it is not native to us. For love comes from God, and all human love is given secondhand. We were loved and now love. We breathe it in, like a forest drinking sunlight, like fish swimming about in a river, unaware at times of its source and deeply conscious of love's divine origins at others. We bask in it, we were conceived by it, for God made us so that He might love us all the more. "We know how dearly God loves us," Paul says with a soul tightly gripped, "because he has given us the Holy Spirit to fill our hearts with his love."[3] Our love for Him is always love in return.

Love began with the cross. It was there when John saw four soldiers nail Jesus's hands and feet, by His consent, and then take His clothes for plunder. He had outer garments that the soldiers split four ways, confirming the prophetic words David had written centuries before, and a robe underneath they did not want to tear. John tells us it was "seamless, woven in one piece from top to bottom."[4] This the Roman guards threw dice for, to see which of them would be the lucky winner. John's imagery is beautifully symbolic of love's divine consistency: stretching from manger to grave and grave to resurrection, from eternity to eternity, we are viewing a single, perfect act of love anchored in Christ's cross.

That seamless robe was paired with garments freely handed over to clothe each of His abusers. For, as Jesus explained, when someone takes your tunic, you give your cloak as well. That is love, and that is the path it took to enter this world.

"What will we eat? What will we drink? What will we wear?" Jesus asked aloud one day.

The questions were rhetorical, and they were not for Him. He was perched on a hilltop, surrounded by thousands of budding disciples who had gathered to hear His impressive teaching. He continued, "These are the thoughts unbelievers fret over, but you don't have to carry them. Your Father knows better than you do how much you need these things. Every bird in the wild looks to Him for provision and finds it. Every lily of the field is clothed by His kind hand."[5]

"Just look at the wildflowers that grow by the road and render the dull grass fuchsia, ochre, and vermillion." He paused and added, "They don't work or make their clothing, yet Solomon in all his glory was not dressed as beautifully as they are."[6]

If King Solomon had been present among the crowd, he would have wholeheartedly agreed. "Like a lily among thorns is my darling among the young women,"[7] he wrote long ago of his wife. "How beautiful you are, my darling! Oh, how beautiful! ...You have stolen my heart, my sister, my bride; you have stolen my heart with one glance of your eyes, with one jewel of your necklace."[8] What was he next to her!

The truth was Solomon was the most exquisitely handsome man the woman had ever laid eyes on, as perfect in character and reputation as he was in rugged physical frame. He was powerful, regal, godly, and rich beyond counting. "I'm just a wildflower picked from the plains of Sharon, a lotus blossom from the valley pools,"[9] she had stammered, blushing at her husband's side. She was utterly captivated by his beauty, as was every other woman at that time looking on jealously.

Yet it was her, his precious dandelion, that Solomon could not turn away from. He did not give a second thought to his own glorious, God-blessed appearance. He did not even remember his storied name in her presence. To him, she was the breathtaking one. Her smile made his pulse race and his heart pound. The scent of her hair and the shimmer of her earrings were what he could not get off his mind. She was the one he loved and longed for.

And her enchanting beauty was the very proof of his deep affection. He had loved her and, in the process, made his sweetheart lovely. All that God had poured on Solomon in blessing, he had channeled into loving her. "I am dark but beautiful," she said to her friends. "Don't stare at me because I am dark—the sun has darkened my skin. My brothers were angry with me; they forced me to care for their vineyards, so I couldn't care for myself—my own vineyard."[10] In his love, Solomon had done for her what she could never have done for herself. "I am my beloved's and my beloved is mine; he browses among the lilies,"[11] she said with a happy sigh.

Solomon was not on the mountain for Jesus's sermon, but the Son of David was, and His heart pounded with that same passion as He looked out. The infant Church sat on the slopes, dotting the grass like spring violets, wrecking His heart. Oh, how He loved her! How He longed for her to know all He had planned!

"Don't worry about a thing, My dear, dear ones. You have nothing to fear. God will certainly clothe you with heaven's finest. This is what He wants to do, and it gives Him such joy. Watch for His King's arrival, and His goodness will come for you too."

His eyes were shining as He spoke. He could picture it already: the Church, His Bride, dressed in dazzling white linen and her jewelry made of hammered gold and flawless pearls. Her arm was delicately threaded through His, leaning on His strength as they glided through their wedding feast. "Oh yes," He said again, "Seek His righteousness and it will come."

Like a Polaroid, the final pages of Scripture give us a single frame of that wedding feast we know as the Kingdom of God. There we see the Bride, us, at last dressed and made ready to run down the aisle. Face to face, we will finally see our Jesus in His full risen glory. But we can rest assured it will be us that Jesus has locked in His sights, mouth slightly agape in dreamy wonder at the staggering Beauty approaching the altar to take His hand.[12]

It is a scene from a fairytale, like a peasant girl transformed into Cinderella, and it is one God Himself will bring about. For our wedding gown is His greatest gift of love and sets the stage for a lifetime of continued kindness with Jesus. That is what clothes represent in Scripture, acts of holy love. Clothes to cover and protect, clothes to arm and defend, clothes to honor and make beautiful, and there is no lovelier garment than the wedding dress of Jesus's Church.

There is a reason this scene comes last, for the Bride can only be dressed in what she has been given to wear. And the Bible is not the story of the Church. It is the story of the one who loved her and gave Himself up for her. It is the story of the Son of David, who in all His brilliant, eternal chabod is not dressed as beautifully as she. It is first and foremost the story of Jesus's robe; for without it, not only would there be no bridal gown, but there would be no Bride.

Jesus spoke candidly about His wedding one night at the home of a prominent Pharisee. He had been invited to dinner, and all the social brass were present, delighted at the chance to see and be seen rubbing elbows with the famous rabbi. He watched as they fought over the prime seats around Him, wrestling and forcing their way into the limelight. Their selfish behavior proved a teachable moment, and He began to tell them what they could expect in the coming Kingdom.[13]

"There was once a great king and his son. The prince was getting married very soon, and the king was sparing no expense for the happy occasion. He had planned an opulent banquet for all his royal guests, with plenty of food and wine and luxurious furnishings. His palace was draped in beautiful decorations to display his vast wealth and even greater joy.

"At last the day arrived, and the king sent his servants out to round up everyone on the guest list. Some inexplicably refused to come, but those that did entered his court one by one, eyes lifted in awe of what they saw. Every corner of the palace was breathtaking. The mosaic floors, the intricately carved walls, the endless supply of refreshments. The sights and sounds were amazing. Each attendee was dressed in their most beautiful clothing, for it is not every day you are summoned to the wedding of the prince!"

That thought must have pleased the Pharisee's guests. One man could not help himself and blurted out, "How fortunate the one who gets to eat dinner in God's kingdom!"[14]

"Yes!" Jesus agreed, and then He continued, "The king looked across the party, beaming. But his happiness suddenly turned to boiling outrage. He marched across the courtyard to where a man stood in rags.

"'How did you get in here dressed like this?" the king demanded. The man was speechless. Before he could even open his mouth, the king called for his guards. "Throw him out!"

No doubt the room froze around Jesus. Jaws stopped mid-chew, tipsy looks sobered up, and perhaps those who had pushed and shoved to sit beside Him were really beginning to regret it.

"The wedding feast will be like this," Jesus said. He meant for the peacocks at the table to think a little less highly of themselves, but the parable was not an indictment against them or a threat they would not be invited. They would most certainly be there dressed in their God-given finery. Jesus would see to that. Rather, the story was about how that very thing could happen, how commoners prone to sin and pride could wind up at the God of heaven's wedding. He, the Bridegroom, was the man in rags whisked away by God's anger, and it was imperative everyone in attendance see it happen.

Love, by its very nature, is costly. To give is to give away, and the more extravagant the gift, the more the giver feels the loss. Love is no exception, though love makes the sacrifice willingly because it feels like joy. Love is remarkably resilient in the face of loss because it does not think of itself. It only cares for the other and gladly goes without.

Love is what motivated Jonathan to abdicate his right to the throne. He was the heir-apparent to King Saul, but he loved David more than himself. He knew God had marked David as His choice to reign over Israel. As a sign of everlasting friendship and humble loyalty, Jonathan dressed David in his own robe, tunic, belt, and weapons. David stood as the crown prince, while Jonathan cheered for his success from the sideline.[15]

Love would later move David to take those kingly robes and crown off in the presence of the Lord and dance with abandon. He worshipped with all his might in little more than underwear as all the kingdom looked on, but David might as well have been the only one there before the Chest of the Covenant. For it was for God alone that He danced, for God alone that He offered up his affections.[16]

Together, the generous lives of Jonathan and David pointed ahead to the night Jesus slipped off into the servants' quarters to remove His clothes. It was Passover, and the disciples didn't notice Him go, not immediately. They were busy enjoying the traditional meal: roast lamb, bitter salad greens, flatbread, and plenty of wine. He quietly left the room and took off His outer garment. He set it down and wrapped a towel around His waist like an apron. He found a shallow basin and a pitcher of water and brought it all back to the table.[17]

Without saying a word, He crouched down by the disciples' feet and began to wash them with the water and bowl. He dried them carefully with the towel He was wearing.

Conversation halted, and the disciples stared down at Him awkwardly. You could hear a pin drop. Every eye was fixed on Him as He made His way around the table.

Foot washing was a slave's task. John, who recorded the moment in his gospel narrative, tells us Jesus knew the terrible events that were about to unfold. This was the Last Supper, and by dawn, He would be on the cross. He knew Judas was about to step out from the meal and sell Him to the Jewish leaders. He knew Satan had worked in the shadows to lure him away. Yet Jesus made no attempt to distance Himself from Judas, or for that matter, all the others who would run off in fear soon enough as well. Judas's feet were among those He gently washed and dried that night.

John says He knew too that He had come from God and was imminently returning to His presence. We might misread that as Jesus knowing He was headed for death. What John actually means is Jesus knew He was God. He knew He deserved far better than anything earth had to offer, and He knew He would soon be reinstalled in the place of highest glory, co-reigning beside the Father Himself. He knew the Father had placed all of creation under His power. He knew the kingly robe, tunic, belt, and weapons were His. He knew that everything He would have upon His return to heaven He had had before and from always. There was nothing to gain personally from His short time in the flesh. If ever there was a moment to indulge or accept honor from people, this meal was surely it. Instead, Jesus took off His God-clothes and crown of laurels to love His friends all the more.

When Peter's turn came, Jesus bent down as He had with the others and placed one foot into the water. But Peter broke the uncomfortable silence that had settled over the Upper Room with a loud protest.

"No, Lord! You simply can't," he cried out, saying what they were all thinking. He drew his dripping foot back, angrily offended. *You're better than this, Jesus!*

"Unless I wash you, you won't belong to me,"[18] Jesus said. "Take the robe, Peter."

So, there He was, the Son of God, with a dirty towel wrapped around His waist, bearing the literal and figurative filth of those He chose to love. Scripture lets us know He put His clothes back on after He finished washing the disciples' feet, but only so that He might hand them over again at the cross and also cover His Gentile executioners. Love for God, love for enemies, love for brothers, mothers, and friends: they are one and the same to Christ.

Those were the rags He took with Him to the crucifixion, given to Him by the will of the Father. He sat back down to the meal and told the disciples things were about to change, but not to worry. "So the world might know how thoroughly I love the Father, I am carrying out my Father's instructions right down to the last detail."[19] And with that, they stood up from the table and walked together out to the Garden of Gethsemane.[20]

The Garden, a serene grove of olive trees just outside Jerusalem's gates, was where they went to pray and await the band of mercenaries who would arrest Jesus.

The disciples watched in disbelief as a mob emerged from the peaceful night and tied Jesus's hands. Peter lashed out with a dagger but quickly dropped it and fled for his life. They all did, every single one of them, abandoning Him into the mist. In the flurry, one disciple even snagged his nightshirt on a branch and ran off naked without it. He is unnamed in Scripture, though Bible scholars have long thought him to be John Mark, author of Mark's gospel and assistant to both Paul and Peter in their missionary journeys. But you and I should see that he is nameless because he is all of us, from Adam and Eve on through to today: naked, ashamed, and running yet again from the Lord in the garden.

Only one man did not run off that night, and that was Jesus. The Father's perfect will held Him steady. "The Father knows you need clothing, dear children," He had told them. 'Do not be afraid, little flock, for your Father has been pleased to give you the kingdom."[21] Jesus stood still and let the arrest unfold. "Seek first His kingdom and His righteousness, and all these things will be added to you as well."[22] It was a plea for His Church to come into alignment with the grand work of God, to trust the righteousness of Jesus alone. To call for the coronation of Christ was to actively pray for the cross and to accept this singularly strange method of redemption, and Jesus was first in line to offer the intercession. "This, then, is how you should pray: Our Father in heaven, hallowed be your name, your kingdom come, your will be done, on earth as it is in heaven."[23] Every line was a direct request for the Father to hasten the cross's coming.

Jesus was led to the home of the high priest Caiaphas, who pressed the Lord hard with questions. They had already made up their minds to kill Him, but they first needed to provoke Him into saying something, anything, that would justify it. Men bribed as witnesses against Him came forward to testify, lying about what He had done and said over the past three years.

Jesus remained silent. The accusations conflicted and canceled one another out, and when Caiaphas saw he was getting nowhere, he went for the jugular. "Are You not going to answer? Tell us straight: are You the Messiah, the Son of God, or not?"

That question Jesus answered. "I Am," He replied. The old man's eyes widened, for he heard exactly what Jesus meant. It was more than he could have hoped for. He had all he needed to publicly condemn Him. In a display of mock horror, Caiaphas grabbed the neckline of the beautiful priestly robe he was wearing and ripped it down the front. "You heard it for yourselves," he shouted to the court. "He claims to be God, and for that He must die!"

He, too, was in desperate need of clothing.

Jesus was immediately ushered from Caiaphas's house to Pilate, the Roman governor ruling over Israel at that time. There, the Jewish leaders repeated the charges and urged for a death sentence, for only the Romans had authority to enact it. When Pilate interrogated Jesus, however, he found no reason at all to support it.

"He has done nothing wrong," he told them. Pilate was no stranger to corrupt politics and could see that the priests wanted Jesus dead purely out of spite. They refused to back down, and even stirred people in the streets to clamor for a guilty verdict. They shouted at riot level until Pilate finally caved to quiet the madness. "Understand that I find Jesus innocent," he announced to the bloodthirsty crowd. "I'm washing my hands of this crime—this is on you. Take this 'King of the Jews' away and crucify Him."

Roman soldiers led Jesus down from the governor to be flogged. The lead-tipped whip cut His flesh to shreds. Bleeding profusely and in almost indescribable pain, he was taken outside to the Praetorium courtyard where the whole regiment was waiting in glee. Jesus was a doomed man and easy prey.

"What a king!" they howled in laughter. One took the scarlet robe off his own uniform and draped it over Jesus's raw shoulders. Another found a vine and twisted it together to form a pitiful crown. "Now He looks the part," he said as he dropped to his knees in a mocking bow. Their cruelty turned violent, as they began to spit on Him and hit Him with a reed cane. When they grew tired of the bullying, they took back the costume and pushed Him out of the courtyard. "Come on, You. Out to the cross."

"How did you get in here without wedding clothes?"[24] the King asked His Son. Do not glance past these words, for they form the single most important question in Scripture. How did Jesus, the perfect, spotless Lamb of God, come to stand in sin-stained rags before the Father? The answer is by obedience, which Jesus said is indistinguishable from love.

Isaiah tells us God foresaw the desperate conditions on earth, saw the havoc our rebellion would wreak on humanity and on every corner of creation, and long before the need arose made the decision to send His Christ:

> *"The Lord looked and was displeased to find there was no justice. He was amazed to see that no one intervened to help the oppressed. So he himself stepped in to save them with his strong arm, and his justice sustained him. He put on righteousness as his body armor and placed the helmet of salvation on his head. He clothed himself with a robe of vengeance and wrapped himself in a cloak of divine passion. He will repay his enemies for their evil deeds. His fury will fall on his foes. He will pay them back even to the ends of the earth. In the west, people will respect the name of the Lord; in the east, they will glorify him. For he will come like a raging flood tide driven by the breath of the Lord."*[25]

The cross was not a surprise to Jesus. We must also understand that it was not His idea. It was the Father's plan, His way to atone for our sin, which Jesus dutifully accomplished. He did not approach the Father to offer Himself unsolicited, nor did He volunteer to liberate us as our Messiah. He came to Calvary when He was sent as God's designee. And when He did, He bore the full brunt of God's fierce judgment. He was the one the fury fell on, for He became God's enemy that day out of perfect, lovingly submissive obedience.

From His birth, He was marked out as the Christ by His clothes. The angels that sang overhead in the night sky told the shepherds they would recognize Him by a peculiar sign. His mother had wrapped His little body snugly with strips of linen to keep Him warm and to comfort His first cries. She laid Him to rest in a manger, probably in a cave doubling as a stable, as the animals housed there looked on.[26]

It was that combination of swaddling clothes and feeding trough that the shepherds were to look for. A newborn, wrapped in grave clothes, laid upon an altar. "He is Christ the Lord!" burst from the constellation of angels.

The shepherds left their fields and raced into town. Bethlehem was not a large place, and they soon found themselves in a stable staring in wonder at Jesus and His young parents. Mary wondered deeply too. The angels' words burrowed into her heart, and when the linen-wrapped baby was sleeping quietly beside her, she asked herself what she was really beholding.

It would come full circle there at the cross, when she stood tearfully beside John and their broken friends. She watched Nicodemus and Joseph of Arimathea take Jesus's lifeless body down. She saw them hurriedly wrap it for burial, wishing to honor Him in death but in a race against the sinking sun. She saw the sheet of linen they had purchased to make strips once again, and the cloth that covered His beautiful face. And then they placed Him in a tomb, rolled a stone to block its entrance, and she saw Him no more.[27]

Patiently, all those who loved Him waited for the Sabbath to pass. They intended to visit His grave at first light to embalm Him properly, to care for Him one last time in the only way they still could. As soon as Sunday morning came, while the sky was still dark, they were awake and active. Spices and jars in hand, they headed for the cemetery.

By the time the women reached Jesus's tomb, gleams of sunlight were peeking over the hills. But the scene was not at all what they expected. Someone else had gotten there first. Someone had already pushed aside the great stone, and the crypt was wide open. The squad of soldiers that had been assigned to guard Him was nowhere in sight. Silently, they peeked inside and discovered that Jesus's body was gone too.

Adding to the mystery, they soon saw the tomb was not wholly empty. Bits of fabric were lying on the rocky floor, those same linen strips the angels had sung over and Mary had wept upon. The face cloth was there too, set neatly to the side, still in the exact place His head was laid on Friday. In an indescribable act of love, they had deliberately been left behind.

Peter and John raced to the tomb in a panic when they heard He was no longer there, not yet realizing He had been resurrected. But when John saw the grave clothes, he believed.

What are we to make of these bits of discarded linen, stained with Christ's dried blood and the dust of a borrowed grave? Holy unto the Lord, they ought to be inscribed, as the High Priest's turban was long ago. The High Priest was required by Moses's law to change out of His priestly garments when His shift in the tabernacle was finished, but Hebrews makes it quite clear Jesus is not yet off the clock:

> *"Now there have been many of those priests, since death prevented them from continuing in office; but because Jesus lives forever, he has a permanent priesthood. Therefore he is able to save completely those who come to God through him, because he always lives to intercede for them. Such a high priest truly meets our need—one who is holy, blameless, pure, set apart from sinners, exalted above the heavens."*[28]

Neither did He leave the strips behind as evidence that He was alive, like breadcrumbs for us to follow. He appeared to people personally for that and left no room for doubt. They talked with Him, touched His scars, and ate meals together. Only John seemed to notice the strips anyway, and together with a fresh reading of the Old Testament, considered them a conclusive sign of who Jesus must be: the Christ.

Jesus had told His disciples a day would come when the Bridegroom was taken from them and they would deeply mourn His absence. That day was now past. "No one tears a piece out of a new garment to patch an old one," He had continued, "and no one pours new wine into old wineskins."[29] Translation: we must let the old go. Get up and embrace what God has done!

The strips were left behind for us, His own clothes we are meant to now put on. They are the wedding dress, if we will have Him as our groom:

> *"When I looked at you and saw that you were old enough for love, I spread the corner of my garment over you and covered your naked body. I gave you my solemn oath and entered into a covenant with you, declares the Sovereign Lord, and you became mine. I bathed you with water and washed the blood from you and put ointments on you. I clothed you with an embroidered dress and put sandals of fine leather on you. I dressed you in fine linen and covered you with costly garments. I adorned you with jewelry: I put bracelets on your arms and a necklace around your neck, and I put a ring on your nose, earrings on your ears and a beautiful crown on your head. So you were adorned with gold and silver; your clothes were of fine linen and costly fabric and embroidered cloth. Your food was honey, olive oil and the finest flour. You became very beautiful and rose to be a queen."*[30]

That is the offer Jesus has laid on the table for us. Like Esther, will we accept this once-in-a-lifetime invitation? Will we run to His palace, let Him dress us, and take the Bride's crown? Will we join Him in this new covenant? Esther stole the king's heart and lived under the protective shadow of his favor the rest of her days. How much greater is the love and eternal devotion God is extending through His Risen Christ![31]

Will I put on the robe? That is the question each of us must answer for ourselves. Seeing the humble strips of linen in an opened tomb, what will I do? John saw and immediately believed. He threw on the wedding gown and let the exquisite love of God wash over him. Divine love takes the form of many garments in our earthly lives: armor for battle, a banner for praise, a crown and ephod for our royal priesthood, an everyday dress of Christlike character; until finally, on that last glorious day, the Bride is ready for the wedding feast, together with the Spirit calling her Great Lover to come.

His is a love that dispels all fear, for it covers all our needs. There is no fear of judgment, rejection, disgrace, or abandonment in the covenant of Christ, if we will receive it. And when we are unable to do even that much, His love will not fail. Love never fails. It will continue to pursue us and show us kindness until we are able to trust it, and then shower us with more. Love "always protects, always trusts, always hopes, always perseveres."[32] That is what God is.

John saw the strips and readily understood: "This is love: not that we loved God, but that he loved us and sent his Son as an atoning sacrifice for our sins...and so we know and rely on the love God has for us."[33] Love for God is merely letting ourselves be His beloved. Peter, on the other hand, needed a little more time. He had been devastated by the cross, and though he believed upon seeing the risen Jesus, he had wounds that needed healing before he could draw close. The strips meant nothing to him, yet for he did not recognize God's love.

A few evenings after Easter, he and John decided to go out fishing. They headed down to the Sea of Galilee where they had been business partners so long before. John's brother James came too, along with Thomas and a few others. Together I imagine they stared at the lake and let the many treasured memories of Jesus's ministry play back: the storms, walking on the waves, crossing back and forth between teaching engagements, the first time they heard Jesus preach. The familiar water looked very different now that He had been raised. Like skewering Leviathan with a harpoon, God had defeated that unruly Sea with resurrection.[34]

The seven disciples pushed their boat out a short distance from shore and settled in for a relaxing night. The sun dipped, and the moon rose over the calm water. Peter, John noticed, took off his outer garments as he fished. Perhaps the air was stuffy or he simply did not want to get his clothes dirty among the bait and tackle, but the Holy Spirit made sure that John took notice.

Peter was naked, spiritually speaking, and hurting. He had not grasped the foot washing or the clothes Jesus left in the tomb. The night of the betrayal, he had sworn by his own life not to let Jesus die, even if it meant Peter died defending Him.[35] Not only had Jesus rejected this sincere but absurd declaration of affection, but He'd also promised Peter that he wouldn't make it to dawn without disowning Him. The Evil One would see to that. "Simon, Simon, Satan has asked to sift each of you like wheat," Jesus said, shaking His head. "But I have pleaded in prayer for you, Simon, that your faith should not fail. So when you have repented and turned to me again, strengthen your brothers."[36]

Peter could only watch as the crucifixion unfolded. He was powerless to stop it and cried bitterly when the prophesy about himself came true. Under pressure, he folded. He denied ever knowing Jesus. Peter cursed His Lord three times to save his own skin, and cringed to see Jesus look up upon hearing it. The curses were the last words Scripture records between Jesus and Peter before He died.

"He was stripped for work,"[37] John poignantly says. Stripped by Satan's vicious sneak attack, stripped by shame and regret, stripped by a sense of total failure, but only so by God's express permission. As with Job, God required Satan to do his threshing within the limits He had personally set. It was painful, and poor Peter was as humiliated as he was baffled in the aftermath, but it was for the colossal good waiting on the far side of the cross. Like Job, Peter hadn't done anything to deserve such cruelty, but it had come for him anyway, and it was thus a very downhearted Peter who sat in the fishing boat.

All that night, the disciples cast nets into the lake but hauled in nothing. When the sun rose, a voice called to them from across the lake. The light was still dim, and they could not make out who the figure standing on the beach was. He cupped His hands around His mouth and shouted, "Catch anything?"

"No," one shouted back.

"Drop your net on the right side of the boat. That's where they are!" came the reply. And when they did, so many fish filled the net they couldn't lift it from the water.

"It's Him!" John whispered in reverence. Twice now they had seen Jesus miraculously bring fish up from the deep. This Sea was brimming with resurrection, for the Resurrection Himself was in command on its shore. At that, Peter threw on his clothes and jumped headfirst into the water. His heart was burning, and he could not wait another minute. He swam in faster than the rest could row straight to where Jesus was standing.

Jesus was ready for him. He had a campfire going, with bread and fish grilling over it, and He invited all His friends to sit down to a hard-earned breakfast.

Peter was stripped, and yet, he still did not understand. What was it he put on, there in the boat, at the sight of Christ? He did not know. His instinct was to jump, and so he made the same well-meaning mistake once more. He dressed and then dived into the sea. Jesus was merely calling him to come, yet Peter again tried to offer a heroic death. After they had finished eating, Jesus pulled him aside. "Walk with Me a minute, Peter," He said.

The two began to walk and talk along the water's edge. After a bit, Jesus pointed at Peter's clothes. They were still damp despite the campfire's best efforts.

"When you were younger, Peter, you could go anywhere and do what you pleased. You could dress any way that you liked," He said. "But now things are going to be different." Jesus looked out over the Sea, like He saw something not yet in focus. Peter tried to follow His eyes but could not tell what it was.

"When you are older, Someone else is going to decide that for you. Someone else will decide how you dress and lead you by the hand where you don't want to go."

Peter did not know what any of this meant. He looked down at his robe, puzzled. Breaking the fourth wall, John graciously steps in as narrator to help. He writes parenthetically, "Jesus said this to indicate the kind of death by which Peter would glorify God. Then he said to him, 'Follow me!'"[38]

Follow Him where? To arrest, into disgrace and condemnation for Jesus's sake? Peter had already attempted that, but Jesus had not let the mob lay a hand on any of his disciples. To combat for His name? No, Jesus had forbidden violence too. To stand bravely against temptation? Peter now knew that was beyond his ability. To the cross, then? No. Jesus had told him quite plainly no one could follow Him there. The Messiah's cross was for Christ alone, and for us vicariously only through faith. What sort of death, then, could Jesus mean? What kind of death could Peter offer to God that would glorify Him? That was his heart's desire.

The riddle would only make sense, many years later, when Jesus's words were fulfilled with uncanny accuracy. By that time, King Herod had unleashed a torrent of persecution against the Church. He had murdered James and thrown Peter into prison to await a mock trial and certain death.[39]

The night before Peter was slated for execution, an angel appeared in the jail cell. Peter had already resigned himself to his fate and fallen sound asleep. He was heavily guarded. Both his arms were chained to a soldier, and fourteen more stood outside the cell to block the door, yet Peter slept like a baby. Perhaps he was even a little glad for another chance to die honorably for His Christ.

The angel came in a flash of bright light and smacked Peter on the side to rouse him. "Get up! Get dressed! Get your coat and let's get going!" he said urgently. The angel removed the shackles from his wrists and led the way.

Peter obeyed, thinking he was dreaming. He followed the angel through the cell door, down the halls, and outside the prison grounds. It wasn't until they reached the city and the angel vanished that Peter realized this was no mirage. He ran to tell those praying for his release that he had been set free. The Church went wild to see his face!

That was the moment it clicked for Peter. Scripture tells us: "Peter finally came to his senses. 'It's really true!' he said. 'The Lord has sent his angel and saved me from Herod and from what the Jewish leaders had planned to do to me!'"[40]

At last, Peter understood that the death of Jesus had come so that he would not die. He had been delivered from the cross by the cross, because the cross of Christ is the definition of holy love. As he slept in that cell, he had looked the part of a crucified criminal: hope gone, robe discarded, his head slumped over as in death, his chained hands painfully outstretched between two guards.

But it was just a resemblance. God had no plan for Peter to die. Twice now, He had intervened to give Peter life. The first was at the cross, despite Peter's attempts to thwart it, where Jesus laid Himself down and purchased redemption for all humanity. The second here recalled the cross to powerfully and personally explain it. This act of sheer kindness allowed Peter to finally understand what he had believed and faithfully preached for so many years. Punch drunk and overjoyed outside that prison, he threw on the wedding gown and ran to the arms of his Bridegroom.

What kind of death glorifies God? Peter knew the answer was Jesus's death. His is the death that does not end in death, neither for Him nor for Peter nor for you and me. His is the death that leads to life, for life is the will of God. I need only put it on to taste the glorious love of God. I will let it work resurrection on my behalf. That is the only death you and I will ever experience, if we dare to accept it, and by our lives in Christ we will glorify our God. I will, shoulder to shoulder with John and Peter and all my brothers and sisters, claim His love. I will receive and wear proudly His love as the bridal robe and crown, for that is my love for Him in return.

"We, though, are going to love—love and be loved. First we were loved, now we love. He loved us first."[41]

---

1 1 John 1:1–2 MSG
2 1 John 3:16 NIV
3 Romans 5:5 NLT
4 John 19:23 NLT
5 This story occurs in Matthew 6 and Luke 12.
6 Matthew 6:28–29 NLT
7 Song of Songs 2:2 NIV
8 Song of Songs 4:1, 9 NIV
9 Song of Solomon 2:1 MSG
10 Song of Solomon 1:5–6 NLT
11 Song of Songs 6:3 NIV
12 This story occurs in Revelation 21.
13 This story occurs in Matthew 22 and Luke 14.
14 Luke 14:15 MSG
15 This story occurs in 1 Samuel 18.
16 This story occurs in 2 Samuel 6.
17 This story occurs in John 13.
18 John 13:8 NLT
19 John 14:31 MSG
20 These stories occur in Matthew 26–27, Mark 14–15, Luke 22–23, and John 15–19.
21 Luke 12:32 NLT
22 Matthew 6:33 NIV
23 Matthew 6:9–10 NIV
24 Matthew 22:12 NIV
25 Isaiah 59:15–19 NLT
26 This story occurs in Luke 2.
27 These stories occur in Matthew 27–28, Mark 15–16, Luke 23–24, and John 19–20.
28 Hebrews 7:23–26 NIV
29 Luke 5:36–37 NIV
30 Ezekiel 16:8–13 NIV
31 This story occurs in Esther 1–10.
32 1 Corinthians 13:7 NIV
33 1 John 4:10, 16 NIV
34 This story occurs in John 21.
35 This story occurs in Matthew 26, Mark 14, Luke 22, and John 13.
36 Luke 22:31–22 NLT
37 John 21:7 MSG
38 John 21:19 NIV
39 This story occurs in Acts 12.
40 Acts 12:11 NLT
41 1 John 4:19 MSG

Picture Four: *Child*

CHAPTER EIGHT

Now He Has Us

"To them God has chosen to make known among the Gentiles
the glorious riches of this mystery,
which is Christ in you, the hope of glory.
He is the one we proclaim, admonishing and teaching
everyone with all wisdom, so that we may
present everyone fully mature in Christ."

– Colossians 1:27–28 NIV

Once, when the disciples were squabbling about which of them would become the most famous, Jesus called a child over to Himself. With the disciples watching (and quite red-faced over their immature argument), He sat down and wrapped His arms around that little one. He pulled her in close and didn't let go. Then He gently told His friends that whoever embraced a child like this was really embracing Him.[1]

That quieted the room. They were ashamed of their bullheaded pride. It had come at the worst possible moment. Jesus had just told them His cross was on the horizon and that His suffering would be immense. But they didn't understand what He meant and shifted to ranking themselves instead.

The disciples were clearly childish, but not in the way Jesus was talking about. He did not mean for them to act like spoiled brats or remain infantile thinkers. He was modeling what He did mean: children who were permanently in His embrace. "Welcome a little one like this," He said, "And you'll be welcoming both Me and the Father who sent Me to you."

Christianity is simply allowing Jesus to do it. It is me permitting Christ to wrap His arms around my tiny, desperately weak self and settling in. I must lean against His chest and melt into those broad shoulders. I must fight the urge to stiffen back up or separate. I must be still, utterly still until the discomfort drops away and He is my home. I must rest, once I learn that I can rest here in safety. I will rest and heal. That is what He is offering to me, to each one of us. I must become a child like *this*, for this is what He has had in mind since before time began. And once I do, I must welcome others. I welcome the one who loved us first when I do. This is welcoming Jesus in return, which is really welcoming the Father our hearts burn to behold and have close.

When we look around at the vast family called the Church, this is what we are really seeing. Every brother and sister of ours is but a little child caught in His embrace, forever paired up with Him. The Holy Spirit says we ought to think of Christ when we see one another, and He does not mean it superficially. "This is Jesus," He testifies, and we are to treat our Lord with honor.

And the same is true for how we are to think of ourselves. We are called to love our neighbor as we love our self. Something astounding happened in that room as the disciples looked on. Before their very eyes, that little child was swallowed up into the greatness of the Father and His Son. They could not possibly understand it. They did not understand that Jesus had to die, even when He had just told them plainly, "The Son of Man is going to be betrayed into the hands of his enemies. He will be killed, but three days later he will rise from the dead."[2] It was like a foreign language to them. But Jesus needed them to understand it, and when plain words failed, He turned to pictures. He wrapped His arms around the little one to demonstrate what His crucifixion would bring about.

"A child like this is Me. Receive it."

There is a name given to Jesus that means *God with us*, the name Immanuel. God promised through Isaiah that a child was coming who would rescue His people from fear. He would not abandon them in their need, not ever. When the angel announced Mary's pregnancy to a shell-shocked Joseph, this was the prophecy being fulfilled: "Look! The virgin will conceive a child! She will give birth to a son, and they will call him Immanuel, which means 'God is with us.'"[3]

He was born to deliver the world from both sin and oppression, to be there with us through the culmination of all God's creative work, human history, and salvation. And John saw the end. It was life, an eternal life shared between God and His people, a family at long last reconciled. The end, which was not an end at all, was God and humanity together living in the same space and holiness. John wrote in his Revelation journal, "I heard a loud voice from the throne saying, "Look! God's dwelling place is now among the people, and he will dwell with them. They will be his people, and God himself will be with them and be their God."[4] Heaven and earth had become one, like two lenses brought into a single focus.

That is Immanuel. That is the work God gave His Son to accomplish, and it is work that is well underway. He is the one who fuses God to His dearly loved world, for Jesus is the *with* Immanuel proclaims. He is the reconciler. He pulls together Father and us—each of God's adopted children, whom He unashamedly mortgaged the heavens for.

The *us* of Immanuel's name is a holy mystery. It is the *us* Jesus put on display that day in Capernaum for the disciples. It is the *us* of Christ and a little child. *Us* is the new creation formed by the sacrifice of Jesus. And it can only be understood by experiencing firsthand the love of Christ to its depths. We must be embraced in order to see what God has done at the cross. The disciples could not grasp why Jesus talked about His death because they had not yet tasted this love. But Jesus knew that soon enough, they would.

The Holy Spirit has tucked a family portrait into the pages of Scripture to help us see Immanuel. It sits there like a fine oil painting hung over the fireplace, showing each component of God with us in detail. One day as Jesus was out teaching, Jairus pushed his way through the crowd and collapsed at His feet. He was an important and influential man, well respected as president of the local synagogue. But pride was not on his mind that day. He began to plead with Jesus, "My daughter, Lord! She's dying, come quick! Come lay your hand on her so she will live."[5]

Jesus did not hesitate. Immediately, He followed Jairus back home to the little girl. Some distance off from the house, however, a messenger met them with terrible news. "Jairus, your daughter is gone," he said. "She's dead now. There's no need to trouble Jesus anymore."

Jesus interrupted before the father could absorb what he was hearing.

He looked him straight in the eye. "Don't listen to that. Just trust Me." Jairus nodded weakly.

When they arrived, family and friends had already gathered around the girl's bedside to mourn. Jesus had no patience for their noisy wails either. "She's not dead. She's asleep! Pull yourselves together!" They laughed at him dismissively. He put everyone but the child's parents outside and slammed the door behind them.

Jairus had picked the right day to call on Jesus, and not because He was unusually testy. Scripture lets us know He had arrived to the area that morning by boat. He had crossed the Sea of Galilee, and we know that the Jesus Jairus met on the shore was far more than the humble teacher who met the eye: this was a revelation of the crucified and risen Messiah. This was Jesus glorified, the Firstborn from the dead.

Jairus, too, was a revelation. The crowd had watched this good man place all his hope in Jesus, even though hope was dead and belief was beyond absurd. This father never wavered in his trust. This was the Heavenly Father broken over us, His beloved, sin-sick, and spiritually dead sons and daughters. He has only ever had one refrain in His heart: "Jesus! Jesus will make it right. Jesus will restore what death has taken."

And so, Father and Son looked down at the little girl lying motionless on the bed. Jairus held his breath, his wife there beside him, as Jesus bent down, picked up the child's limp hand, and clasped it in His own.

"Talitha koum,"[6] He said tenderly. "Dear girl, it's time to wake up!" Still holding His hand, she sprang to her feet. Imagine how quickly Jairus threw his arms around her, around them both, and began to sob with a hundred different emotions. It was still nothing compared to how fast our Father's embrace comes to scoop up the *us* of Jesus and His forgiven child.

"The child is sleeping," He had told the mourners. She was no more dead than He was. United to Him, how could she be? He was brimming with resurrected life, and now so was she.

But just so that no one missed what had really happened, He instructed her elated mother and father to give her some food. He would make the very same request for Himself on Easter, when the disciples were slow to believe He was really up from the grave and present in flesh and bone. "Do you have anything here to eat?"[7] As they stared at Him, terrified and trembling behind locked doors, He ate a piece of broiled fish to prove He was no phantom. Feeding Jairus's daughter was a powerful sign, not that she was well enough to be hungry, but that that same resurrected Lord was alive within her.

Immanuel. Father cradling the *us* of Christ and Jairus's only daughter. That same *us* is what ruined Paul forever. He had been a violent man, a persecutor of the church, but on his way to make arrests, he ran headlong into the Lord and was literally knocked off his high horse. He fell to the ground and tasted the grace of God. In three days, he too went from a dead man to a resurrected child.[8]

Under the Holy Spirit's tutelage, he came to realize the Jesus who fiercely loved him was also powerfully alive inside him. Jesus was reigning in heaven and somehow also right there within him. Slowly, it dawned on him that Christ was making up all the gaps. Where Paul blatantly opposed God, there was Jesus. Where Paul unknowingly fell short, there was Jesus. Where Paul tried his best and failed, there was Jesus. Where Paul died, there was the living Jesus! Jesus had not only removed his sins; He made Paul perfectly righteous. Paul no longer bothered with trying to be good. The righteousness Jesus provided was infinitely better. And Jesus was making up for every other shortcoming, insecurity, and need he faced. What was left for him to do? It was a watershed moment for the apostle as he unpacked what was going on under his skin:

> *"When I tried to keep the law, it condemned me. So I died to the law—I stopped trying to meet all its requirements—so that I might live for God. My old self has been crucified with Christ. It is no longer I who live, but Christ lives in me. So I live in this earthly body by trusting in the Son of God, who loved me and gave himself for me. I do not treat the grace of God as meaningless. For if keeping the law could make us right with God, then there was no need for Christ to die."*[9]

All that was left, he decided, was to admit what had happened. He had died.

The day Paul met Jesus on the road, he was led by the hand into the city limits of Damascus. The brilliant vision of Jesus had struck him temporarily blind. Paul was deeply shaken, scared to death the Lord would retaliate for all the cruelty he had shown the Church. He fasted and prayed his tail off not to be squashed like a bug. God heard the prayer, probably with a smile, and sent Ananias to restore his sight.

Paul gladly took the mercy, placed his faith in Jesus, and was baptized on the spot. "I have been crucified with Christ," he at last understood. That baptismal water was not a bathtub; it was a cross transfigured into a sea, Christ's cross. He realized that by believing in Christ, he too had shared in His crucifixion. That was the point where Jesus wrapped His arms around Paul and *us* was created. Paul continued his thought: "...If we have been united with him in a death like his, we will certainly also be united with him in a resurrection like his."[10] We can be sure that once Jesus has a child in His embrace, He does not let go, even in death and on through to the other side. It meant Paul came out of the tomb when Jesus did, sharing in the resurrection. He literally now lived by faith that the Son of God was raised.

Paul reveled in that truth. Every second going forward, Jesus would be the one doing the heavy lifting. It would be His righteousness on display whenever the Father searched Paul's heart. It would be Jesus's joy that made Paul strong, and Jesus's mind that Paul learned to think with. Jesus would be Paul's confidence in facing poverty and abuse and in coming before God boldly in prayer.

Ironically, embracing *us* gave Paul the absolute freedom to be himself. Not the old self he once was, but the new creation Jesus had made him into and had always had in mind. He found the paradoxical promise of Jesus to be wonderfully true: "Whoever finds their life will lose it, and whoever loses their life for my sake will find it."[11] He had found the real Paul.

Like bolt cutters, it removed all the anxieties that bound his hands and feet. No longer did he have to wonder if he was diligent enough in obeying the Law or holy enough to tiptoe around God's throne. He could pursue any career, live in any country, eat any food, and associate with any people he liked. He could stop obsessing about his physical flaws and limitations. He could enjoy his time in God's presence, knowing that it was Jesus who opened the door for him and Jesus who kept it propped wide. Paul could sleep easy, suffer much, and shrug off any criticism that tried to wreck his peace. Best of all, he could accept himself exactly as he was, for Christ provided everything he lacked. He had answers for every worry and could finally live.

I had become *us*, Paul's supreme treasure. He understood that Jesus's presence in his life did not make him less, as if something wrong was happening by needing Christ continually. There was no more pressure on him to get his act together spiritually, for *I* was dead. Christ now lived, and Paul lived by faith in Him.

Paul is certainly not the only one in Scripture to experience the glorious mystery of Immanuel, though he may have been the first to put words to what was happening theologically. God with us is the gift of God to every believer, and not just those born since Jesus entered the world. Paul was practically giddy to realize the whole swath of His people, from the beginning of time up to this very day, have access to Christ's *with* through faith. Past or present, he marveled:

> *"People are made right with God when they believe that Jesus sacrificed his life, shedding his blood. This sacrifice shows that God was being fair when he held back and did not punish those who sinned in times past, for he was looking ahead and including them in what he would do in this present time. God did this to demonstrate his righteousness, for he himself is fair and just, and he makes sinners right in his sight when they believe in Jesus."*[12]

Snapshots of Immanuel fill the Old Testament, pointing ahead to the riches we who know Christ by name possess. We can see Him in Obed, the miraculous baby born to Ruth and Boaz. But no one thought of Obed as theirs alone. After his birth, all the old women in town crowded around and cooed, "Naomi's boy!" over his tiny fingers and perfect pink cheeks. Naomi was the grandmother, Ruth's former mother-in-law. She was mother to Ruth's first husband who had sadly passed away before they could have children. Ruth had remarried into the same family, and by God's law, newborn Obed was legally reckoned as belonging to Naomi's dead son. Obed received all his property as his heir. He was also listed in Boaz's family tree as his true son. Naomi happily cradled Obed in her arms. Like the neighbor women said, she was holding both her grandson and the son she had lost simultaneously.[13]

Laughter was the name given to Abraham's son Isaac.[14] He too was

Immanuel. Abraham and Sarah waited nearly a century to meet him, but God had promised they would laugh, and He does not break a promise. At the age of ninety, Sarah at last gave birth. And there she was, nursing an infant and giggling until her sides hurt at this ludicrous wonder. "What will others make of this!" she said, grinning. She rocked him gently and broke into the lullaby she'd been saving all those empty years. She traced each feature of his face with a wrinkled finger. "Women everywhere are going to join in on this Laugh," she whispered with a holy hush. She knew Isaac was the fulfillment to a far greater promise, one so massive and God-sized every generation on earth would be blessed through it. This one son of Abraham was also God's one Son, the rightful Heir to all of God's goodness and covenants. Lest we misunderstand, Paul makes it crystal clear that Jesus was there too in Sarah's embrace, born to inherit and to be our incredible inheritance: "Notice that the Scripture doesn't say "to [Abraham's] children," as if it meant many descendants. Rather, it says "to his child"—and that, of course, means Christ."[15] Jesus would make *us* joyfully real across time and history. All of *us* will laugh.

And when David faced off with the fearsome giant Goliath, he shouted:[16]

> *"You come to me with sword, spear, and javelin, but I come to you in the name of the Lord of Heaven's Armies—the God of the armies of Israel, whom you have defied. Today the Lord will conquer you, and I will kill you and cut off your head. And then I will give the dead bodies of your men to the birds and wild animals, and the whole world will know that there is a God in Israel! And everyone assembled here will know that the Lord rescues his people, but not with sword and spear. This is the Lord's battle, and he will give you to us!"*[17]

Goliath saw only a boy in shepherd's dress on the battleground, but David says it was the Lord. He says it was the Lord who then put a stone into a sling, took aim, and let it fly with bullseye accuracy. He was telling the truth, for when Goliath crumpled to the ground, it was by the hand of Jesus. David, like Paul, had joined to Him by raw faith. He too had been crucified with Christ. He had climbed down into that valley for battle, a metaphor for death, and thereby linked Himself forever with his God. He had met Jesus at the cross, and the result was *us* standing on the valley floor, rippling with power, authority, and ready for war.

Unfortunately for the giant, Goliath knew none of it. He had no idea David was invincible the moment he stepped into the valley. He had no idea he was staring down the God of the Angel Armies. He thought he was looking at a mere child. He paid for that arrogant ignorance, for only a moment later, David climbed back up from the valley holding Goliath's severed head in his hands. That is resurrection at work.

David knew what had really happened, and King Saul saw it too. He had met David many times before in his court, but the boy was now somehow utterly unrecognizable. He stared at David, perplexed, and asked his general, "Whose son is this young man?"[18] He knew the son of Jesse alone had not won this victory.

Us is our permanent condition in Christ, and we must learn to live out the new reality of Immanuel. Going forward, every day of this life and the next, we must allow ourselves to rest in His arms so that the truth will fully permeate our thoughts and actions: I no longer live; Christ lives in me.

Consider how drastically this impacts worship, ministry, and that most intimate relationship of all, prayer. I have died, and it is the Son of God now dwelling here instead. So, when I draw into the Father, it is Christ He is actually seeing. I am present too, but only because I live in Jesus by my faith. Christ, not I.

In this arrangement, prayer becomes exactly what Jesus said it should be, a conversation between Father and Son. This is the prayer that is always heard and always answered with a yes.

Jesus so simplifies prayer in His teachings that it is easy to mishear Him. He compared prayer to a little child asking for a snack. We would be greatly mistaken if we thought we were the child who has this access and privilege! Instead, Jesus said, our part in prayer is like a man caught in a lurch when a guest came to his home:

> *"Imagine what would happen if you went to a friend in the middle of the night and said, 'Friend, lend me three loaves of bread. An old friend traveling through just showed up, and I don't have a thing on hand.' "The friend answers from his bed, 'Don't bother me. The*

door's locked; my children are all down for the night; I can't get up to give you anything.'"[19]

The answer was a frigid no! He had a good reason to bother his neighbor, but Jesus is clear that asking for the right things and being good do not count for anything in prayer. They won't rouse our Neighbor or trigger His generosity. Something more is needed to open God's hand.

Jesus must have had a twinkle in His eye as He spoke because that *Something* was standing right in front of His listeners. He continued: "But let me tell you, even if he won't get up because he's a friend, if you stand your ground, knocking and waking all the neighbors, he'll finally get up and get you whatever you need."[20]

If a good reason and a cordial relationship are not enough, what does it take to put bread in our human hands? It takes Someone getting up from the dead of night to open the door—a resurrection, Christ's resurrection, which we claim by faith. We must knock as *us*, and never on our own, proclaiming the Risen Christ present within us. He must be the one the Father sees. Jesus tells us to knock voraciously like this until our God can stand it no more. Every rap on His door cries out, "Papa, Jesus! Look down and remember Your covenant!" We have Jesus's word the Father will give His Son whatever He needs, and we might well see the whole neighborhood raised up in the process.

It is the presence of Jesus that makes all the difference. He is the Son, and we must claim and pray from this one posture alone. That is what it means to ask in Jesus's name. We must pray as *us*. To go to the throne without Him is to face God in our own sin and shabbiness, at our own great peril.

The story of Shadrach, Meshach, and Abednego provides a stark reminder of what would happen, should we dare to try it. When Israel was taken into captivity by the Babylonian empire, these three were taken as well. For some time, they enjoyed comfortable lives in their new country but soon found themselves crosswise with Nebuchadnezzar, a powerful king with an explosive fuse.[21]

They were given an immediate death sentence. Soldiers bound them hand and foot and threw them into a furnace to be burned alive. But to everyone's amazement, the furnace did not kill them. Shadrach, Meshach, and Abednego were completely fine inside it, walking freely through the blistering flames. The court officials squinted through the fire and, as if things weren't strange enough already, counted an extra man. Somehow, another had appeared beside them. Nebuchadnezzar exclaimed to his aides, "Look! I see four men walking around in the fire, unbound and unharmed, and the fourth looks like a son of the gods."[22]

He commanded them to come out from the furnace and stand before him. They did, showing no sign of char or smoke on their skin and robes. He was in awe, canceled their executions, and promoted them to high positions in his kingdom instead.

It was not the men's stubborn allegiance to the Lord that changed Nebuchadnezzar's mind, nor their adherence to kosher laws, nor their record as good servants and model citizens that impressed the fuming king. Nothing about Shadrach, Meshach, and Abednego made any difference. It was the presence of the Son of God in the fire that dramatically changed the king's thoughts toward them. He saw the fourth individual was no ordinary man, and in a heartbeat, flipped from fury to favor toward the other three.

It is but a shadow of the love the Father lavishes on His children when we come as *us*. Why would we come any other way? When the Father sees His Son, He instantly responds. Sin is forgiven, and mercy flows. He is eager to bless, to be kind, and to provide whatever is needed. Come into His throne room by Jesus's name, using that name only, because you believe Christ is kneeling down and asking the Father with you. Immanuel is present, and we must claim Him.

Prayer that leans entirely on Jesus is the only kind He taught us to offer because it is the only kind that works. He told the disciples:

> *"Pray like this: Our Father in heaven, may your name be kept holy. May your Kingdom come soon. May your will be done on earth, as it is in heaven. Give us today the food we need, and forgive us our sins, as we have forgiven those who sin against us. And don't let us yield to temptation, but rescue us from the evil one."*[23]

This is first and foremost a child's prayer, a prayer of the Son before His loving Father. Only He can pray it, which is why He instructs us to begin "*our* Father," meaning His and mine, His and yours, ours, presenting God right away with faith that claims the rock-solid certainty of *us*. Every item that follows on this prayer list is steeped in that reality, asking in the context of *us*. Everything, from the most mundane task of finding bread to seeking protection in the midst of spiritual warfare, is rightly situated in Jesus by praying *our* Father. We can only pray as *us*.

Take heart that a union with Jesus does not end in the asking, nor even once God responds with His answer. The burden does not shift over to you and me after the prayer session closes and the regular day resumes; *us* remains for the outward facing life too. God equips *us* through prayer to live and do good in this world, and He has no intention of you and me going out alone.

This is very good news, because one of the most daunting challenges we face is staring up at us from the middle of the Lord's Prayer. Jesus threw in a couplet that would freeze us on the spot were we to rise from the altar and attempt to do it on our own: "Forgive us our debts, as we also have forgiven our debtors."[24] He might as well have said, "Father, You can go ahead and forgive me, because all my relationships are humming along. I have obeyed You perfectly and forgiven every single person who has wronged me. I qualify for Your mercy but do not need it."

In case the insanity of this petition was lost on His original listeners, Jesus spelled it out with additional gravitas: "If you forgive other people when they sin against you, your heavenly Father will also forgive you. But if you do not forgive others their sins, your Father will not forgive your sins."[25]

Surely, we see that this is a prayer no one can begin to make alone. Who can come to God confident they have extended forgiveness on a divine level, to every person and for every circumstance, no matter how deeply we were hurt? We do not even know all the wrongs that have been committed against us! If the Father will not forgive us until we have done this work, which Jesus solemnly assures us is the truth, if we cannot even lift this prayer to Him until we are sure we've done our part, what good is He to us? And if by some miracle I did find myself worthy to pray it, wouldn't that make me spiritually perfect? What would I need Him for? What would be the point of Jesus's sacrifice? Would that mean I can come to God through my own righteous efforts, or even more troubling, that He expects me to?

Paul said absolutely, unequivocally, positively, *no way*. "I do not treat the grace of God as meaningless. For if keeping the law could make us right with God, then there was no need for Christ to die."[26]

We can be certain that if Jesus is commanding us to pray to *our* Father about forgiveness, it is because only by *us* can it happen.

God is well aware that forgiveness is beyond humanity ability. And when Jesus encountered embittered hearts during His ministry, He did not demand they do the impossible. He told them stories so they could see.

"There was once a man who had two sons," He said to the crowd. Around Him was an odd mix of prostitutes, thieves, swindlers, and Pharisees. Jesus had become a haven for sinful rabble, and that had prompted the ire of the meticulously religious Pharisees. The mercy He generously gave out only made it more difficult for these teachers to get past the others' many, many wrongs.[27]

Jesus proceeded to tell them the story of the Prodigal Son, the younger of that man's two boys who threw away his inheritance in a foreign country. Penniless, disgraced, and out of better options, he crawled home to his father to beg forgiveness. But to his complete surprise, the father was so glad to see his child he ran out to meet him on the road. He kissed his face and wrapped his arms around him. Jesus continued:

> *"His father said to the servants, 'Quick! Bring the finest robe in the house and put it on him. Get a ring for his finger and sandals for his feet. And kill the calf we have been fattening. We must celebrate with a feast, for this son of mine was dead and has now returned to life. He was lost, but now he is found.'"*[28]

Everyone listening would have recognized the story immediately. It was the story of Isaac and his twins, Esau and Jacob. Jacob had tricked his father into giving him Esau's inheritance. Esau was the older of the two and the legal recipient to the larger portion of Isaac's estate. But Jacob, taking advantage of his father's poor eyesight, had dressed in his brother's robe, ring, and sandals and pretended to be Esau. He had made his father a feast while Esau was away, snatched the blessing, and gone on the run to avoid his brother taking revenge.[29]

Jacob fled to a foreign country and spent twenty hard years in exile. He worked for his uncle, who was cut from the same deceitful cloth. During that time, he married four bickering women and had at least thirteen children, most of whom he did not love or want. He became very wealthy as a shepherd, which attracted his uncle's repeated attempts to sabotage his wages. Working conditions were miserable, and he was extremely unhappy. When he could stand no more and his heart longed to return home, God assured him it was time to head back to his father.

He set out for Canaan with all his wives, flocks, and children in tow. The only problem was Esau. Though it had been two decades, Jacob was terrified his twin was still out for blood. And sure enough, it was not long before his fears were realized and Esau came riding out to meet him on the road. Jacob braced for the worst.

But it was a vastly different Esau who arrived that day. He ran straight toward Jacob, weeping with joy, and embraced his long-lost brother. Jacob stood tense in his arms, not trusting them. He tried to offer Esau bribes from his herds. Esau would not take them. The kisses were genuine.

"Jacob," Esau said, waving off the gifts. "Welcome home! Keep the animals! Keep everything!" There was not a hint of bitterness left.

Jacob marveled at what was unfolding. "Brother," he began, studying Esau closely. "To see your face is like seeing the face of God."[30] He was completely shocked by the transformation.

Jesus tells us there was a good reason Jacob thought he saw someone else. Esau looked an awful lot like the Father in that moment, because Esau had become *us*. It really was the Father opening His arms to His wayward younger son, because Christ had Esau squarely in His.

How had it happened? Esau certainly did not feel this way at first. He had been cheated and robbed of his blessing, all while obeying his father as a good son. The injustice smoldered into murderous threats against Jacob and poisoned his relationship with Isaac. Jesus told the crowd:

> *"The older brother stomped off in an angry sulk and refused to join in. His father came out and tried to talk to him, but he wouldn't listen. The son said, 'Look how many years I've stayed here serving you, never giving you one moment of grief, but have you ever thrown a party for me and my friends? Then this son of yours who has thrown away your money on whores shows up and you go all out with a feast!'*"[31]

Esau was not capable of forgiving Jacob on his own. None of us are. To God, forgiveness means canceling debts, whatever their size, and then paying the debt He says we owe to them! That is to pay them back in mercy, grace, and goodness. The problem is, of course, you and I have nothing with which to pay them. We were robbed.

Forgiveness does not mean pretending nothing happened. God does not ever intend for us to stuff down hurts or accept pain. Instead, He says to pray, "Forgive *us* our debts, as *we* forgive our debtors." If there is an *us*, then what is left to be forgiven? *Us* is my declaration of faith before the Father that Christ has covered every debt by His cross, including how I was wronged and the impossible kindness I owe my many wretched brothers and sisters. *Our* debts are settled. I need only claim it by this prayer.

Everything hinges on *us*. There must be an *us* before I ever set out to pray it, and by the grace of God, Jesus has taken the initiative. He was standing before the Pharisees, before the tax collectors and prostitutes, before the disciples, all in their various bitter, selfish, and boneheaded conditions, so that they would see. He would go to the cross to bring Immanuel about, even though no one yet understood. And when He rose from the dead, He would open His arms and offer the embrace of *us* as the *with* to "my Father and your Father, to my God and your God."[32]

Child of God, who are you? Who are we that have put our hope in Him? We are the *us*. We are new. In ways we can only begin to comprehend, we are not who we were before salvation. You may look down at your hands and feet and gaze at your face in the mirror. You may see no change. Your thoughts and behaviors may be unaltered, and that might even disappoint you, but you must look beyond the physical and grasp what has happened with faith. There is only an *us*.

What are we once we have been born by the Spirit? Something wonderfully grand, something so magnificent it defies taxonomy. Paul says we have become an entirely new kind of creature that never existed beforehand. Let the hugeness sink in: children of God are new works. *Us* is not found in Eden, when God crafted the human race from clay, nor at any point during the billions of years He took to form the stars. We are something new and something far greater. We, His children by faith, are

His masterpiece, the pinnacle of everything God ever wanted to accomplish through creation. Eden was merely the backdrop. We are His very best idea and proudest achievement. "Therefore, if anyone is in Christ, the new creation has come: The old has gone, the new is here!"[33]

We are so new, so spectacular, that God says the universe pales in comparison. We make the Milky Way seem dim, and like a new father, our God cannot take His eyes off *us*. We are His beloved, the subject of His songs, and when any wicked spirit dares to challenge His greatness, He does not justify His name. He merely points to *us* to prove His brilliance. We are His eternal boast against hell and that He is God: *us*, His redeemed. Hear Him laugh with pure joy over us:

> *"'I will say to the north, "Give them up!" and to the south, "Do not hold them back." Bring my sons from afar and my daughters from the ends of the earth—everyone who is called by my name, whom I created for my glory, whom I formed and made... You are my witnesses,' declares the Lord, 'and my servant whom I have chosen, so that you may know and believe me and understand that I am he. Before me no god was formed, nor will there be one after me. I, even I, am the Lord, and apart from me there is no savior. I have revealed and saved and proclaimed—I, and not some foreign god among you. You are my witnesses,' declares the Lord, 'that I am God. Yes, and from ancient days I am he. No one can deliver out of my hand. When I act, who can reverse it?*[34]
>
> *'Forget the former things; do not dwell on the past. See, I am doing a new thing! Now it springs up; do you not perceive it? I am making a way in the wilderness and streams in the wasteland. The wild animals honor me, the jackals and the owls, because I provide water in the wilderness and streams in the wasteland, to give drink to my people, my chosen, the people I formed for myself that they may proclaim my praise.'"*[34]

Child, do you realize your very existence glorifies God? He is the Creator. We were the culmination of His first word: "Let there be!" We were made in His image. With Jesus, we are new creatures and grafted directly into His family tree. We are His heirs. We need to look on our own lives, our own selves and miraculous bodies with more amazement than we feel in the presence of the Northern Lights and the Amazon. Look at the detail in your skin tone and how your eyes catch and interpret the light. Marvel at how you run or swim or how the pencil in your fingers transcribes your thoughts. Praise God for how your stomach can metabolize a meal and your heart can hear His holy voice. Yes, and praise the Father for the nickname He's given you: Christian, a name redolent with love meaning "little Christ." That is who we have become, who we are, who we are most like. We are with Him. Praise God for placing the value on your life as Christ. You were worth Jesus to Him. You still are.

You were the joy awaiting Christ beyond His cross. You, Child. You were what He saw beyond it. His joy is to give you life and to live it with you, to be the *with* for you to know the Father. To have you and for you to have Him. That is why God emptied His coffers and poured out all He is. Life is worth all this to Him. Life *with* us.

Child, to live, to really live in Christ, is to glorify the Creator. Simply *being* is carrying out the Father's design. Live out Immanuel. There is no question of whether we have done enough to please Him. *Us* now exists, which is what He always wanted. You have been given life to live on God's level. Inherit the earth! Sing! Play! Eat! Go in this direction, or that. With Jesus, it is all blessed and brings honor to our Father.

---

1 This story occurs in Matthew 18, Mark 9, and Luke 9.
2 Mark 9:31 NLT
3 Matthew 1:23 NLT
4 Revelation 21:3 NIV
5 This story occurs in Mark 5, Matthew 9, and Luke 8.
6 Mark 5:41 NIV
7 Luke 24:41 NIV
8 This story occurs in Acts 9.
9 Galatians 2:19–21 NLT
10 Romans 6:5 NIV
11 Matthew 10:39 NIV
12 Romans 3:25–26 NLT
13 This story occurs in Ruth 1–4.
14 This story occurs in Genesis 17, 18, and 21.
15 Galatians 3:16 NLT
16 This story occurs in 1 Samuel 17.
17 1 Samuel 17:45–47 NLT
18 1 Samuel 17:55 NLT
19 Luke 11:5–7 MSG
20 Luke 11:8 MSG
21 This story occurs in Daniel 3.
22 Daniel 3:25 NIV
23 Matthew 6:9–13 NLT
24 Matthew 6:12 NIV
25 Matthew 6:14–15 NIV
26 Galatians 2:21 NLT
27 This story occurs in Luke 15.
28 Luke 15:22–24 NLT
29 This story occurs in Genesis 27–33.
30 Genesis 33:10 NIV
31 Luke 15:28–30 MSG
32 John 20:17 NLT
33 2 Corinthians 5:17 NIV
34 Isaiah 43:6–7, 10–13, 18–21 NIV

CPSIA information can be obtained
at www.ICGtesting.com
Printed in the USA
LVHW112332060922
727629LV00003B/144